US Nuclear Bombers

By Peter G . Dancey

Acknowledgements

The photographs used in this work have been collected over more than a decade since the author began aviation writing in 1995 and, unfortunately, I cannot remember with any great accuracy the origins of some. A number are from defunct Part Works, all the others are as detailed. To all contributors I express my many thanks in particular to those persons I have been unable to contact.

Front Cover:
Strategic Air Command B-52 Stratofortress 0026 stands 'alert' ready to go at it's US base during the 'Cold War'.

Rear Cover:
A B-52H with it's massive brake-chute deployed lands back at Diego Garcia following a mission during Gulf War II in 2003, low on fuel, it's 'pogo' outriggers now well clear of the ground

Developed from the British EE Canberra B.2 Tactical Air Command nuclear-capable Martin B-57 'Canberra' light bombers became totally committed to the war in south-east Asia and served the USAF well while suffering high attrition in that theatre.

CONTENTS

Foreword
Introduction

Copyright © 2008 Peter G Dancey

ISBN 978-0-946995-62-2
Galago Books 42 Palace Grove Bromley BR1 3HB England

Printed and bound in Great Britain by Biddles Ltd., King's Lynn, Nofolk

Foreword

Since 1947, when Strategic Air Command (SAC) possessed 319 Boeing B-29 Superfortresses, the USAF's strategic bomber force has remained the world's most powerful strike arm. Having taken control of the 40th Bomb Group (BG) in the Pacific theatre in WW II as a Major-Gen, post-war it was General Curtis E Le May who passionately believed that America must have the ability to inflict total devastation on any potential adversary, to such an extent any act of aggression made against the United States would be met by an equivalent strike on that aggressors industry and population. Fortunately, whilst the situation that prevailed with the Soviet Union post-WW II deteriorated into the Cold War, and much aggressive posturing by both sides occurred at times, sense prevailed and World War Three was avoided and there is no doubt, this can be largely attributed to the strength of SAC and its nuclear bomber fleet, supplemented from the 1960s by Intercontinental Ballistic Missiles (ICBMs).

While both east and west held hundreds of long-range bombers in their respective inventory's, the doctrine that held good in the Second World War, that bombers could bludgeon their way to the enemies targets, changed rapidly. General Le May worked on the basis that single or small groups of aircraft would undertake the nuclear mission. Consequently, millions of dollars were spent on developing advanced equipment to counter the Soviet air, missile and radar threats, while crew training and states of readiness placed huge demands on both aircrews and ground-crews of SAC and its much smaller RAF Bomber Command V-Force counterpart. SAC for many years maintained a state of 'airborne' readiness, initially at high altitude and later at low level, with their Boeing B-47 Stratojets and B-52 Stratofortresses. Supporting them were the in-flight refuelling tankers, at one time 600 of them.

While the Boeing B-47 Stratojet and short-lived Convair B-58 Hustler came and went, the B-52 continued on full-time alert throughout the last four decades of the 20th century. It was on nuclear stand-by during the Cuban missile crisis of 1962, it flew conventional tactical and strategic missions in Vietnam between 1965 and 1972, attacked Iraq during both Gulf Wars, Yugoslavia in the late 1990s and the Taliban and al' Qaeda in Afghanistan in 2001-2.

Since the late 1970s, the B-52 fleet has been supplemented by the Rockwell B-1B Lancer swing-wing bomber, the much refined development of the cancelled B-1A. The arrival of the advanced B-1B, meant that SAC at last had a modern aircraft able to deliver either conventional or nuclear weapons as well as stand-off air-launched cruise missiles, though the B-52s also now have this capability. In 1988, in an attempt to thwart the evermore capable Soviet defence radars, the angular Northrop B-2 Spirit stealth strategic bomber entered service. This unique flying-wing bomber made its combat debut in the Balkan war and subsequently in Gulf War II in Iraq.

Advanced avionics, weapon systems and stores, airborne counter-measures, decoys, chaff and flares, have all helped to ensure the USAF manned bomber continues to be the prime element of US strategic air power.

Peter G Dancey
MK 2007

Introduction

Boeing Aircraft, established on 5 August 1933, built interesting modern aircraft; the M.200 Monomail, the all-metal B-9 prototype monoplane bomber, the Model B.247 airliner and the P-26 "Pea-shooter" fighter for the USAAC. Having survived the Great Depression, in early 1934, total manpower at Boeing reached 1,700, but in 1935 dropped to only 600. Boeing was on the verge of bankruptcy. The aircraft which actually saved the company from extinction was the B-17 Flying Fortress bomber in late 1935. The USAAC ordered 13, and Boeing built a big new plant especially for production of the B-17 at Seattle. Subsequently, other aircraft such as the Boeing 307 Stratoliner, M.314A Clipper flying-boat, etc served to reinforce the Boeing name and of course the company. The most prestigious in WW II was undoubtedly the B-29 Superfortress long-range heavy bomber. Eventually used to deliver the thermo-nuclear devices dropped on Nagasaki and Hiroshima, to end the Second World War in the Pacific. That the B-29 secured the company's future is without doubt, as in the first nine months of 1939, it was showing a loss of $2,500,000. At this time, naturally Boeing's fortunes hinged on the military and their big bomber requirements.

With its founder gone, and no passengers or post to transport, the Boeing Aircraft Company concentrated on aircraft manufacture, designing them to the highest innovative standards to increase demand. The new chairman, one of Boeing's original supervisors was Clairmont L. Egtvedt, an engineer and draughtsman. Under his guidance the company produced larger and more luxurious aeroplanes. To meet demands for an aircraft to cross the oceans, Boeing built the Model 314 flying boat, the first long-haul ocean-crossing airliner, capable of carrying seventy-four passengers by day or fifty in overnight sleeping accommodation. It was nicknamed the "Clipper" after the great ocean going sailing ships of the earlier pioneering days. Passengers aboard the Pan Am Clippers crossed the Atlantic or Pacific in style. Seated in spacious salons gazing out of large panoramic viewing windows whilst being served gourmet meals. Also on board these luxurious flying boats were dressing rooms, beds and even a bridal suite. The Model 307 Stratoliner that followed offered even greater luxury, with greater comfort in the pressurised cabin, which meant the aircraft could fly higher and faster, more economically at altitudes 'above the weather' with less turbulence.

With the clouds of war gathering once again and with a new man at the helm, William Allen, the company's former senior lawyer, Boeing turned their attention to manufacturing huge numbers of B-17 Flying Fortress and B-29 Superfortress bombers. History literally repeated itself and the company put their factories at Seattle and Wichita, Kansas, on a war footing and in 1942, it built another plant near Seattle at Renton. From July 1940 to August 1945, Boeing Seattle built 6,942 B-17s and 380 A-20s. At its wartime peak the company employed a total of 78,000 people.

Early in 1941, the US Navy had placed an order for 57 Boeing PBB-1 patrol flying boats. However, at the time Boeing did not have the resources or the capacity to produce these as all the plants were busy building aircraft for the army. As a result the navy decided to build its own plant 10 km south of Boeing, on the side of the lake, near the small Renton airfield. The ground was broken on the 38.5 hectare site on the 2 September 1941. But after Pearl Harbour the US Army, requested a new plant to produce the B-29 Superfortress bombers and finally the US Navy ceded the Renton Plant to the Army in June 1942. The first phase of the plants construction was finished in March 1943 and preparations for B-29 production were started immediately. 998 B-29s and 2 C-97s were built by VJ Day, and after, a further 121 B-29s until June 1946. After which, the plant was closed, and returned to the US Navy, who were to use it as a storage facility.

Meanwhile, in the spring of 1941, the US Government began building Government Plant 2 (Plant 1 was the Stearman works). The new plant was adjacent to existing Boeing operations at Wichita, Kansas. On completion, the plant with a 120,000 m2 covered area, built Boeing B-17 assemblies and 750 WACO designed CG-4 gliders and on the 15 April 1943, the first series production B-29 Superfortress was rolled out at Plant 2. By December 1943 personnel at the plant totalled 29,795. The plant had brought together 29,000 farmhands, housewives, and shopkeepers turned airplane builders, who in 1944, found themselves working 10 hour day and night shifts, six days a week.

Soon, in order to instil a degree of enthusiasm in the workforce, bolstering pride in producing quality output, the Boeing management devised a method of appraising all workers at Wichita. It borrowed a 770 kg bronze plated bell from a town church and rang it every time a new Boeing B-29 rolled off the production line. Army security officers were horrified and ordered the bell ringing to cease forthwith. According to their thinking the sound of it must be reaching enemy ears, somewhere, and could inform the enemy of the B-29 production rate. However, Boeing management liked the bell idea as a morale builder, and informed the security officers that the idea had originally stemmed from Lt Gen. Knudsen, Army Chief of Production. A compromise was worked out. The bell remained, but thereafter was sounded very softly for Boeing employee ears only. With these and other productivity boosting methods the company squeezed what normally would have been a six year program into just two years ! Many aircraft were delivered directly from the drawing board with production development and experimentation moving forward simultaneously.

With the cessation of hostilities in Japan on the 5 September 1945, an order was given out that all operations would be discontinued at the end of todays shift ! All temporary wartime staff; farmers and housewives should return to their homes. However, over the next few months the greatly reduced workforce did eventually deliver the last of the 1,634 B-29s to be built at the Wichita, Kansas plant.

In the autumn of 1946, the Government closed Plant No 2 with employment at Wichita falling to only 1,000 personnel. In 1948, a further 1,000 workers were reinstated to assist with the B-29 modernisation programme. 173 aircraft were modernised, many as tanker aircraft. Continuity of employment for those re-engaged was ensured when Wichita was tasked with similar updates to the uprated B-29D redesignated Boeing B-50.

At the time of the post-WW II formation of the USAF in 1947, the Boeing B-29 was still America's principle long-range bomber. The design dated back to 1938 when studies began for a high-altitude, pressurised bomber with a tricycle (as opposed to a tail-dragger) undercarriage for service with the USAAF in WW II.

Despite the enormous technical difficulties that had to be overcome to meet the air force requirements, the project was approved and three prototype XB-29s were ordered from Boeing, the first flying on 21 September 1942. Fourteen pre-production YB-29s followed and the first series aircraft was accepted by the USAAF in September 1943, armed with five gun turrets and crewed by up to twelve personnel.

Production ceased in 1946 after 4,221 had been built. The type operated in the Pacific where sixty-one squadrons flew the type against Japan and in 1945, the two atomic bombs on Hiroshima and Nagasaki were dropped by B-29s, *Enola Gay* and *Box Car*. Russia too operated a few 'captured' machines that had forced landed on Soviet territory, and Tupolev and the Myasishchev bureaux produced a reverse-engineered copy, the Tupolev Tu-4 Bull. The Shvetsov team worked on producing a copy of the Wright R-3350 Cyclone 18 engines, giving rise to the Soviet-built ASh-73TK piston engines. Other teams copied the many complex systems of the American strategic bomber, including its system of low-drag remotely-controlled gun turrets. It is quite remarkable that the task of copying this airplane that was so far in advance of anything in the Soviet Union at this time, was accomplished in a remarkably short time scale, even though numerous problems occurred at the final assembly stage when, due in the main to US/Soviet measurement standards conversion errors, even the tyres did not fit the wheels. The first Tupolev Tu-4 was built at the aircraft factory at Kazan in 1947.

It first took to the skies in the spring of 1948, though it was not in fact a true prototype but the first of 20 pre-series aircraft, and production deliveries began in 1949. The main difference between the American B-29 and Soviet B-4 (Tu-4) was that the latter airplane had heavier defensive armament, 23-mm cannon replacing the 0.5-in machine-guns of the Boeing aircraft. About 1,200 Tupolev Tu-4s were built (847 by 1952), of which around 400 were supplied to China. Two dozen Soviet VVS heavy bomber regiments operated them during the first post-WW II decade.

Post-war most of the USAAF B-29s were stored, but the Korean War forced the USAF to despatch nine squadrons of Superfortresses for operations against the North Koreans and their Chinese compatriots. At the same time 70 (later increased to 88) ex-USAF B-29s and B-29As were taken out of storage and modernised before entering service with the RAF as an interim bomber pending delivery of the English Electric Canberra jet. The B-29s given the British name 'Washington' entering service in 1950 under the American Military Aid Programme (MAP) for Europe which was initiated as a result of the 'Cold War'. However, by December 1954, the B-29 had been withdrawn from bomber use, the type continuing instead, in the in-flight refuelling role as the KB-29 and weather reconnaissance plane as the WB-29 until 1960, when the type finally retired for good.

In the quest for higher performance Boeing installed four 3,500hp Pratt & Whitney R-4360 Wasp Major turbo-charged engines in a B-29 airframe. Designated XB-44 this flew on 25 June 1947, giving a top speed of 392 mph and the USAF ordered a production batch of 79 under the B-50A designation. With a crew of eleven, distinguishing features compared with the B-29 included a taller fin and rudder for better directional stability and larger intakes below and behind each engine. Subsequent models were the higher weight B-50B of which 45 were built, the D with a longer nose and external fuel tanks under the wings

(222 built), and the unarmed TB-50H bomber crew trainer (24 built).

In June 1943, the USAAF published a request to the American aircraft companies, asking for design feasibility proposals on a multi-engine turbojet-powered aircraft for high-speed, high-altitude photographic reconnaissance and bombing missions.

In contrast to German development and operations of turbojet aircraft, such as the WW II Messerschmitt 262 jet fighter and Arado Ar 234 'Blitz' single-seat bomber with two Junkers Jumo 004 jet engines, the USAAF's first turbojet aircraft was, the Lockheed YP-80A Shooting Star fighter, that did not fly until 9 January 1944.

The USAAF did not publish its requirements for a multi-engine turbojet bomber until 17 November 1944. It was to have a range of 3,500 miles, a service ceiling of 45,000ft, and a maximum speed of 550 mph. Earlier in 1944, the USAAF had requested feasibility studies on such an airplane. The Boeing Aircraft Corporation submitted an independent design proposal, based on a scaled-down B-29 *Superfortress* bomber powered by four turbojet engines, mounted in twin nacelles under the wing and designated Boeing Model 424.

Boeing soon revised its proposal as the Model 432, which repositioned the four turbojet engines inside the fuselage over the main fuel tanks. However, this was not a safe location for the engines, close to possible fuel fume leaks from the main fuel tanks, which obviously if ignited, could blow up the aircraft !

The Model 432 eventually became known as the Model 448, XB-47 of which two were built, albeit without the many design refinements needed for it to enter series production. However, following studies of requisitioned German documentation on swept-wing technology, Boeing altered the XB-47's wings from a straight to swept-wing configuration., giving rise to the Model 450.

The upgraded XB-47 design incorporated a 35° swept-wing and decreased wing thickness to reduce air drag and the number of engines was increased to six by placing two in the fuselage, forward of the tail, although this arrangement was subsequently abandoned. The end of the Pacific War on 15 August 1945, led to the termination of Boeing's major contract for B-29 aircraft and this released considerable manpower to work on the XB-47 jet. After much work, the six-engined Model 450-1-1, with paired engine nacelles under the wing and the third close to the wing-tip, was unveiled.

By October 1945, the USAAF approved Boeing's XB-47 design, authorising two prototypes in December, and releasing funding in April 1946. Boeing engineer's continued to refine the XB-47s design, including tandem two-wheel landing gear arranged on the aircraft's centre-line and retracting into the lower fuselage, outrigger wheels (required for ground taxiing stability) retracting into the under-wing and dual engine nacelles for the inboard pair of powerplants. The in-line centre-positioned main landing gear created a nose-up attitude for maximum lift during the critical take-off phase of flight, which was necessary due to the poor thrust of early turbojets.

By the end of 1955, sufficient B-47 Stratojets were available for the piston-engined B-50 to be withdrawn from front-line bomber duties and re-assigned to reconnaissance (RB-50), weather-reconnaissance (WB-50), and tanker (KB-50) missions. The last of the B-50 series aircraft was retired in 1967.

Chapter 1   Boeing B-29 & B-50 Superfortress

In January, 1940, the US War Department requested a long-range bomber that could fly at 325 mph with a range of 3,000 miles, and deliver 20,000lbs of bombs as well as defend itself; a 'super flying fortress'. Among the major manufacturers competing for the contract was, Boeing Aircraft, who had been working on just such a project since 1937 (Model 341). The Army Air Corp ordered 250 of the new bombers, even though they only existed on paper. Design work proper had been initiated in June, 1940, after the (R-40B Spec XC-218) specification had been issued in the previous January. The aircraft was similar in size to Boeing's earlier giant, the abandoned (Model 294) XB-15 heavy bomber prototype. Whilst only a single example was built the XB-15 did play an important contribution to the development of the B-29 Superfortress. The Model 316, that followed was twice as heavy. Much of the weight stemming from the armour protection for the twelve crew members and other combat equipment. In January 1939, Boeing started design of its Model 333 with tandem engines, tandem bomb-bays and two pressurised crew compartments connected by a tunnel, and tail guns. The Model 333 was refined into the Model 334-A, with higher wing loading, the first real ancestor of the M 345 B-29.

By August, 1939, the M 334 had given rise to the M 341, with its 64 sq/ft wing loading, a 12 man crew, and 2,000lb bomb-load and a range in excess of 5,000 miles. Work started on a full size 'mock-up' (at Boeing's own expense) in December 1939.

However, in April, 1940, the specification was revised to include, leak-proof tanks, more armour, and heavier calibre machine-guns and cannon. Resulting in the Model 345 with its four Wright Cyclone 18 R-3350 twin-row radials, four retractable turrets (with twin machine guns), and cannon in multiple turrets, pressurisation giving an equivalent pressure of 8,000ft altitude up to 30,000ft and the capacity to carry a 2,000lb bomb-load over a range in excess of 5,300 miles at a speed of 400 mph. A maximum bomb-load of 16,000lb, a twelve man crew (the pilots, navigator, bombardier, flight engineer, and radio operator, with three gunners and a radar operator in the aft section), and a tricycle undercarriage. The Model 345, that could mange only a projected speed of 382 mph, had a wing-span of 141ft 2ins and was 93ft in length. Boeing submitted their design to the Army Air Corp (USAAC), project officer Captain Putt as the XB-29. Air Material Command was directed to negotiate for two prototypes and 200 series aircraft.

On 24 August, 1940, the USAAC decided on the Boeing design, and signed a contract for development and production of the two prototypes at a cost of $3,615,095. Lockheed withdrew from bomber design, although Consolidated developed its XB-32 in parallel. The Boeing design was by far the best with ten gun defensive armament in four remotely-controlled power operated turrets and a single directly con-trolled tail turret. In November 1940, Boeing received an order for the third and fourth prototype airframes for static tests.The first engineering drawings were issued on 4 May 1941 and a works order was issued calling for the first aircraft by August 1942 (fifteen months). A 'mock-up' was ready by May 1941..!

Along with the conditional contract issued on 17 May, 1941, a number of changes and modifications were requested. Boeing were to build 250 B-29s and an additional 335 B-17s. Subject to expansion of the Wichita, Kansas facility to meet production targets of sixty-five B-17s a month by July 1941, and twenty-five B-29s a month by 1 February, 1943. Plant expansion at Wichita started on 25 June, 1941, around the nucleus of the plant of the Stearman Aircraft Company, which had become a wholly owned subsidiary of Boeing in 1939.

Following the Japanese attack on Pearl Harbour; the US Air Staff, on 31 January 1942, ordered 500 B-29s and $53 million worth of spares. By then, the world was mobilised in global warfare. The west was certain the Pacific War would be protracted and brutal, fought over vast reaches of ocean. If the Allies were to take the war to the Japanese homeland, the B-29 Superfortress - with its increased bomb-load, ceiling and extremely long-range - was indispensable. Wartime aircraft were to be fitted with emergency rated 2,430hp Wright R-3350-23A engines, cabin pressurisation and remote control of the ten 0.50-in calibre machine-guns and one 20mm cannon. In February, 1941, a production programme was produced by military and industrial personnel. It specified, Boeing - Wichita would produce B-29As, Bell Aircraft Co. would also build B-29s at a new plant to be erected at Marietta, Georgia, (now the Lockheed C-130 plant), North America Aviation (a Division of General Motors) was to build B-29s at its Kansas City plant, and General Motors, Fisher Body Division would produce B-29s at a new plant to be built at Cleveland, Ohio. Wright would supply the R-3350 engines.

In August, 1942, (after the Battle of Midway), a number of planning changes took place. The Army and Navy shuffled projects and plants at two locations, Boeing at Renton, Washington, and North American Aviation at Kansas City. The Navy took over the Kansas City plant. The Army, Renton. The Boeing Sea-Ranger, a prototype naval flying-boat was cancelled to free the Renton production lines. North American at Kansas was tasked with building the companies own B-25 Mitchell bomber, some for the Navy. Fisher Body was withdrawn from B-29 production plans, producing instead, the P-75 fighter and Glenn L Martin & Co., at the Omaha, Nebraska, plant was given Boeing B-29 production. With the all up cost of a B-29 estimated at $1,000,203 and 50 cents. !

The Boeing Superfortress went into limited production by mid-1942, and in early September, 1942, the first XB-29 was towed out of the final assembly hall and flight crews ran up the engines and undertook taxi-tests and a few days later further fast taxi-tests were undertaken and the aircraft became slightly airborne (15ft) three times. The XB-29s official first flight took place on 21 September, 1942, by a crew headed by Eddie Edmund T. Allen. The flight lasted for approximately one hour 15 minutes and general first impressions were good. The second prototype (XB-29) flew almost exactly three months later on 30 December, 1942. But, less than two months later it had crashed, a burning wreck, with Allen and the flight test crew loosing their lives. A fire had started in the No.1 engine (the first of many engine fires), burning through the wing structure.

Tupolev Tu-4 Bull — Soviet B-29 Stratofortress reverse-engineered copy

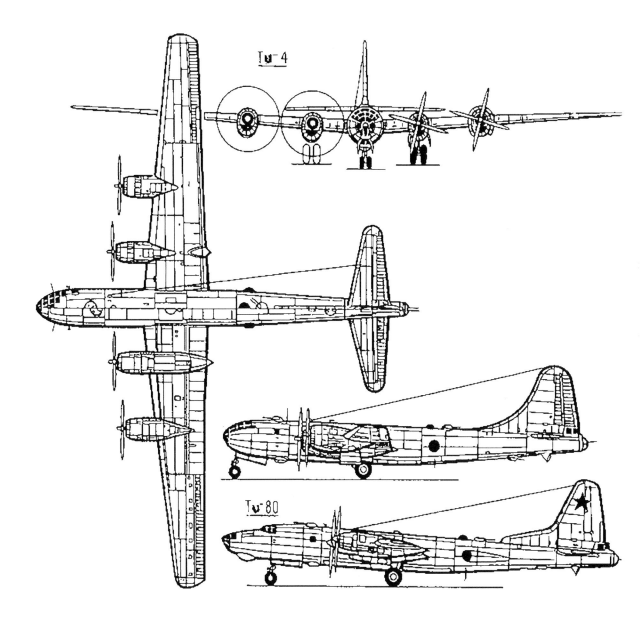

Originally designated B-4, this copy of the Boeing B-29 was put into production in the post-WW II Soviet Union as the Tupolev Tu-4 it was the country's first post-war long-range strategic bomber.

Subsequently, the engine faults were rectified and Sperry remotely-controlled gun turrets fitted to the second XB-29 were replaced by General Electric turrets in the third prototype that flew on 16 June, 1943, and in July the first of 14 pre-production YB-29s were delivered to the USAAF, seven aircraft from the Wichita, Kansas, plant. Only the three XB-29 prototypes were built at the Boeing Seattle plant. All series aircraft were produced at one of four plants, Renton, Wichita (Boeing), Bell's Marietta, and the Martin, Omaha plant. It was the largest single aircraft programme of WW II.

Also in June 1943, the service Superfortress unit, the 58th Bombardment Wing (Very Heavy), started to receive the initial production aircraft. By the end of November 1943 the 20th Bomber Command was formed to take control of the Superfortress units forming at airfields in Kansas. This rapid entry into service meant that many of the airplanes teething problems had not been resolved, however. The most serious of these centred around the Wright R-3350 engine, a newly developed 18-cylinder radial rated at 2,200hp which suffered frequent failures which more often than not led to serious fires.

It is interesting to note that aircraft (B-29A) built at the Renton factory had a decreased fuel capacity by 250 gallons due to the wing centre section construction (five piece wing section). Boeing, Wichita, delivered 175 standard aircraft by the 1 March, 1944. Most were delivered to the 58th Bomber Wing (BW), but unfortunately they were not combat ready and had to be extensively modified, off the production line. By February, 1945, 1,000 B-29s had been delivered, and by March, 1945, production from the Wichita plant alone was, 100 per month. In July 1945, Wichita was producing more than four aircraft a day. In January, 1945, the Bell plant had commenced delivery of 311 radar-equipped (AN/APG-7 Eagle) B-29B aircraft for night precision bombing, some with defensive armour reduced to reduce weight, and the two or three .50-in tail-guns sighted with the aid of a AN/APG-15 radar to deal with enemy night fighters. Contracts awarded stood at 6,289, with deliveries to continue into 1947.

By the war's end sixty-one squadrons of B-29 Superfortresses were activated with the 20th Air Force in the Pacific, and with an equal number being prepared to equip the redeployed 8th Air Force. The total of 3,960 Superfortresses having been delivered by 1946, with the aircraft remaining to form the back-bone of the USAF's Strategic Air Command deterrent force in the early post-war years. With some nine B-29 squadrons deployed throughout the Korean War. A number of B-29 'Washingtons' were supplied Lend-Lease to the RAF as an interim measure whilst the service awaited delivery of its first jet-bomber, the English Electric Canberra.

In addition to WW II series production there was an extensive modification programme and for some time all of the country's modification centres were involved in B-29 work. At the Army Air Force's modification centre at Birmingham, Alabama, almost 9,000 employees were assigned to B-29 Superfortress work. Many problems were experienced with the Wright Cyclone 18 engines of all variants. XB-29 (prototypes) fitted with R-3350-13, YB-29 (P-P models) fitted with R-3350-21, (SP models) fitted with R-3350-23/23A and B-29A fitted with R-3350-57. The engines were so troublesome they were often referred to as the 'Wrong' engines or flame-throwers. They constantly ran 'hot' on the ground necessitating redesign of cylinder baffling and cowl flaps. They were also prone to 'swallow valves. Post-war most of these problems were resolved, but in WW II in the Pacific on one night alone, at Saipan five aircraft of 313th and 58th Bomb Wings had engines catch fire on take-off.

Ironically, the final aircraft to leave Saipan after the war had its No.4 engine burst into flames on take-off. The powerplants that did function correctly were fitted with Hamilton-Standard Hydromatic four-bladed propellers of 16ft 7in diameter (XB-29s were 3-bladed of 17ft diam), with constant-speed governors and hydraulic pitch changers for feathering. Towards the end of WW II some aircraft were fitted with Curtiss electronic propellers with reverse-pitch to assist braking.

Electronic equipment in early B-29 models comprised AN/APN-4 LORAN System linked to a long-range Nav-Aid (Grid System). Later models were fitted with APN-9 (RCA) or the APN-4 (Philco). The aircrafts main bombing Nav-Aid was the AN/APQ-13, a joint development of the Bell Telephone Laboratory and the Massachusetts Institute of Technology (MIT) - it used a 30 inch radar antenna, mounted in a hemispherical radome, installed between the bomb-bays (sometimes this installation was 'touched out' of wartime photographs)

The AN/APQ-13 gave a 360° PPI console display facilitating improved navigation. The AN/APQ-7 'Eagle' bombing-navigation radar was developed by the MIT's Radiation Laboratory and at Bell Telephone. It was built by the Western Electric Co. The 'Eagle' radar was installed in a wing-shaped housing underneath the belly of the aircraft, spanning 17ft it had a chord of 31ins and was just under 8 ins thick. As built, the forward section was a white plastic radome and the rear section was of conventional aluminium. In operation the whole unit was painted black as was the rest of the aircrafts under-belly. Later in the war a number of the 315th Bomb Wing aircraft were fitted with a gun-laying radar, built by the General Electric Co. This radar helped with the operation of the tail-guns. It was mounted in a ball-shaped radome, below and completely outside the tail turret.

The SCR-729 interrogation radar had a paired antenna, one a double dipole type and the other a whip, one on each side of the aircraft nose near the navigators and flight engineers position. Built by Philco the SCR-729 was used to determine range and bearing of any aircraft it might interrogate. The SCR-718C radio altimeter, built by RCA was primarily used on a bomb run to determine the aircrafts absolute altitude above the ground. Most B-29s flew with a crew of eleven. Five officers, the aircrafts commander and pilot, co-pilot, bombardier, navigator, and flight engineer, and six enlisted men comprising, radio operator, radar operator, central fire control gunner, left and right gunner and tail gunner. Later two additional officers, called 'Ravens' flew to operate the ECM equipment.

Post-war, a number of RB-29 'Ferret' reconnaissance variants (redesignated F-13A) were used in the Cold War to monitor Soviet surveillance radar developments, and probe the air defences from Wrangel Island to the Kamchatka Peninsula. There were also a number of SB-29A 'Super-dumbo' search-and-rescue conversions. With fourteen hours duration, it had a under-belly lifeboat installed.

The first F-13 was converted at the Denver Modification Center, and assigned purely for training, to be passed down from squadron to squadron as they deployed overseas. Of the remainder 31 were converted at Boeing Wichita, the remaining 88 (84 F-13A and four TF-13A) at Boeing Renton.

By the end of 1943, it was decided that the B-29 would not be used in Europe but would instead equip the newly formed 200th Bomber Command in India for raids on Japanese targets. In spring 1944, four B-29 Groups of the 58th Wing comprising the 40th, the 444th, the 462nd and the 468th, moved to Kharagpur north-east India to form the 20th Air Force, the direct flight from the United States involving a distance of 1,200 miles, and aircraft had to climb to altitudes around 20,000ft to cross the Himalayan mountains. The initial raid in theatre being flown on 5 June against railway yards at Makasan, near Bangkok. Ninety-eight aircraft made the 2,000 mile round trip. Some 14 aborted and five crashed due to technical problems and another five due to other problems, while only 18 bombs actually landed in the target area.

To enable the B-29, whose combat radius was then only 2,575 km (1,600 miles), to strike Japan, the bombers used airfields in unoccupied China as staging posts — a tactic which involved the bombers in ferrying enormous quantities of fuel, ordnance and supplies to the Chinese bases. En-route lay the Himalayas, the highest mountain range in the world, and the wear and tear on the bombers on these 'Hump-crossing' logistic flights was considerable. Many aircraft were lost due to overheated engines, and crews considered the ferry trips more hazardous than the combat missions to Japan themselves.

It took two weeks to transport sufficient fuel and other supplies to the airfields in China to mount the Yawata mission. The first strikes against the Japanese mainland made from Chengtu on the night of the 15/16 June 1944 when B-29s bombed the Imperial Iron and Steel Works at Yawata on the island of Kyushu.

On 13 June B-29s began to deploy to their forward operating bases. In total 92 bombers set out from India, one was lost en-route and 12 others were forced to turn back. On the afternoon of 15 June, 68 Superfortresses took off to attack Yawata. Each bomber was loaded with eight 500lb bombs plus fuel for a round trip of some 2,400 miles, the longest aerial bombing raid yet made. Lt Tom Freidman, a radio counter-measures officer with the 40th Bomb Group, recalled: "We were scheduled to reach the target around midnight and attack singly, so there was no attempt to assemble in formation. During the long approach flight I moved into the waist gunner's position to gaze out at the scene of ancient China spread out below me in the late afternoon. As dusk fell I crawled back to the windowless, crowded radar compartment, to my position in the aircraft. The countermeasures equipment had been a late addition to the B-29's equipment inventory and, in spite of its great size, there was little spare space, inside the pressurised crew compartments. The racks for my equipment had been squeezed in between the bulkhead and the chemical toilet. As the twelfth man in the aircraft, my 'seat' was the lid of the toilet itself — a subject for numerous wisecracks on the appropriateness of my position from the other crew members."

En-route the target it was obvious as the American bombers had neared enemy territory they had been detected by Japanese Army Tachi 6 surveillance radar. In fact they were aware their approach was monitored for several hours and having crossed the Chinese border, the signals became decidedly stronger, especially as the aircraft passed directly overhead the early warning radar sites. The question was of course what did the Japanese intend to do about the approaching armada of B-29s.

As the bombers passed over the Strait of Tsushima they began to align themselves for the bomb run. For the actual attack the crew were fully attired for combat. Over their overalls, they had so much equipment they could hardly move: Mae West sea survival jacket, parachute, emergency kit, pistol, canteen, flak suit and flak helmet. Once over the target, the Yawata Steel works and the achorage beside it, the radar/bombardier 'toggled' the bombs at the aiming point and in under a minute the big bomber swung on the opposite heading for home.

On return to base at Chengtu the bombers had been airborne for more than fourteen hours. Of the 68 Superfortresses that set out, one crashed on take-off, one crashed on the way to the target and four turned back early Those bombers that reached the target area found the works covered with 5/10ths cloud on top of a layer of industrial haze. Fifteen crews carried out visual reconnaissance on the steel plant and 32 crews bombed the works using radar for greater precision. Post-strike reconnaissance revealed little damage to the works, though several bombs fell on nearby industrial and business areas. Two aircraft attacked the secondary target at Laoyao and five bombed targets of opportunity, while six aircraft suffered mechanical failures that forced their crews to jettison their bombs.

Six B-29s suffered minor damage from flak over the target. Crews noticed that the Japanese anti-aircraft fire was of moderate intensity and generally inaccurate, and that air defence gunners tended to wait until the airplane was totally illuminated by the searchlights before they opened fire.

There were sixteen reports of crews sighting Japanese night fighters, but only five of these resulted in a firing pass on a bomber and none suffered hits (at the time the JAAF had no radar-equipped night fighters in service). It was clear to the B-29 crews that the Japanese night defences on the homeland were no better than those encountered over the occupied territories.

Seven bombers were lost during the mission, all due primarily to accidents or mechanical failures. Enemy action played a contributory part in only one of the losses; on its return flight a bomber suffered an engine fire and made a forced landing in Chinese-held territory, and was destroyed on the ground during a strafing attack by Japanese combat planes.

At this time, the Superfortress was too new and it suffered too many teething troubles for it to achieve much during the initial attacks. Moreover, the forward operating bases in China, reliant on air-supply could not support a sustained bombardment operation. B-29s made only nine attacks on Japan from bases in China before these operations ceased in January 1945.

Subsequent long-range strikes against Japan, post-target Yawata that continued to be made from China, suffered a fairly high casualty rate, due to the combination of the long distances to be flown over enemy territory, navigational and other equipment problems. Many B-29s were abandoned in the air or crash-landed in occupied China. But, the 58th Wing continued to operate from their Chinese forward landing fields right up until March 1945.

During these operations, three B-29s having been damaged, were diverted to Russia, where, as that country was not then officially at war with Japan, they were interned. From these machines, Tupolev produced a 'Chinese copy,' the Tu-4 Bull. In Russia the Bull became the basis for various other developments including the Tupolev Tu-70 troop transport and enlarged Soviet post-war turboprop-powered bomber designs, such as the renowned Tu-95 Bear series.

The initial attack on the Yawata Steel works failed to impress the Japanese military dictatorship. What it proved to the US 20th Bomber Command 'top brass' was, for the B-29 to operate to its full potential, the bomber had to have a well-supplied base within 1,600 miles of its target. For attacks on the enemy homeland no such base existed until Saipan, Tinian, Rota and Guam islands in the Mariana group had been captured, and airfields there extended to accommodate B-29s. The attacks from the new bases began in November 1944 and built up rapidly in ferocity until they very soon laid to waste most of the Japanese wartime industry. This chain of events set in motion by the largely ineffectual first probing raid on the Japanese mainland attack on Yawata.

After US forces captured the Mariana Islands, which lay in the Pacific south south-east of Japan, they built five B-29 bases there — one on Saipan, two on Guam and two on Tinian — each large enough for a 180-aircraft wing and all the B-29s of the 20th Air Force were based in the Marianas. Tokyo was first attacked by bombers from Saipan on 24 November 1944, when Brigadier General O'Donnell's 73rd Wing (the second B-29 Wing to be formed) bombed the Musashima aircraft factory. All Japan would soon come to fear the dreaded 'Bni-Ju's' (B-29s).

On this and other missions from the Marianas the Superfortresses made high-altitude daylight attacks with limited success, but from 9 March 1945 a switch was made to low-altitude night operations using incendiary bombs. The reduction in operating altitudes, avoiding climbs to 7,600 metres (25,000 ft) or more, enabled fuel loads to be reduced and a larger war load carried instead; as enemy opposition was expected to be weak, this was further exploited by the removal of all armament and gunners, except the tail position. The first of the low-level, nocturnal fire raids was directed against Tokyo, which was attacked by 279 Superfortresses with devastating effect : no less than 41 square kilometres (15.8 square miles) of the heart of the city was almost completely burnt out and over a million people — one seventh of the capitals' population — rendered homeless. More than 80,000 people were killed and over 100,000 injured — higher casualties than for either of the two atomic bombs.

The 20th Air Force's campaign against Japan, which included both day and night attacks in the ensuing months, not only caused tremendous direct damage but was also responsible for the withdrawal of many Japanese aircraft from other Pacific theatres for 'Defence of the Homeland' operations. This, in turn, might have become a serious threat to the B-29 operations had it not been for the fact that, following the capture by the Americans of Iwo Jima and, later, Okinawa, the bombers were given the benefit of fighter cover.

Throughout late 1944 and early 1945 the B-29s continued high level daylight raids on Japanese targets but without much success. Losses too were becoming prohibitive. Then in March 1945, Major General Curtiss E LeMay, who had arrived in the China-Burma-India (CBI) Theatre the previous August, to command the 20th Bomber Command (BC) in India, decided to completely change tactics to those that were used with great success by the 8th Air Force in Europe. LeMay, who in January 1945 also took over the 21st Bomber Command (and command of the 20th Air Force in July 1945) put the best and most experienced radar operators in the 21st BC lead planes to act as Pathfinders designated to mark the targets. LeMay reasoned that as the B-29s could not hit their targets accurately, they should area bomb using incendiaries to burn up large areas of the country.

The first B-29 low-level incendiary attack on Tokyo took place on the night of the 9-10 March 1945. Crews were astonished to be told that they were going to fly to the target, each bomber by itself and go in at 9,000ft at night ! Two hundred and seventy-nine B-29s followed the Pathfinders across Cape Noijima, north over Tokyo Bay and across Tokyo at altitudes ranging from 4,900 to 9,200ft. Each B-29 carried eight tons of M69 incendiaries to drop to the pattern set by the Pathfinders. The M69s were set to burst at 2,000ft altitude each in turn dividing into 38 separate sub-munitions covering a swath of Tokyo 500 by 2,500ft with burning gasoline. To B-29 crews it looked like 'the whole world was on fire'. The firestorm consumed so much oxygen that those who did not die by the flames simply suffocated. Almost 16 square miles of Tokyo was razed to the ground as gusting winds whipped up the flames and over 80,000 Japanese died. A total of 14 B-29s were lost and 42 received flak damage.

Despite the losses and the strain on the airmen and ground crews, LeMay scheduled a further five fire-bomber missions in ten days. It was the beginning of the end for Japan, her industry and her people. Throughout early 1945 in addition to the raids on the mainland, attacks were also made on her environs and oil refineries. For attacks on the refineries, B-29 Superfortresses in the 315th BW based on Guam were stripped of all armament except the tail turret, and AN/APQ-7 Eagle radar bomb sights were installed — the radar antenna housed in a 14ft 'wing' under the fuselage. Another unit, the 313th, carried out highly successful aerial mining of Japanese coastal waters and shipping lanes.

As the Japanese fighter units struggled to get sufficient airplanes in the air, to head-off the waves of B-29 bombers it was possible to improve the aircrafts speed by deleting gun turrets and sighting blisters. LeMay wrote: "in the daylight runs, even during the last three months of the war, Japanese fighters would bother us occasionally — diving into the formation, dropping phosphorous bombs, or trying to ram the B-29s — but we'd bother them back. On the 7 May mission for example, our gunners shot down a hell of a lot of fighters — 34 to be exact. We positioned our fighter escorts out in front and made them stay there. This forced the Japanese fighters to attack from the rear, where the compensating gun sights of the B-29s would handle them."

In addition to the bombing raids by up to 500 aircraft, B-29s also carried out extensive mine-laying in Japanese waters, while others including F-13A reconnaissance planes, were employed on photographic reconnaissance missions.

Then, on 6 August 1945, the B-29 *Enola Gay* of the 509th Bombardment Wing (Provisional) operating from Tinian, in the Marianas, ushered in the age of atomic warfare when its bombardier Major Tom Ferebee released the first operational atomic bomb, on the city of Hiroshima. The city was totally destroyed and over 78,000 people killed out of its total population of 348,000. An additional 51,000 people were reported injured or missing.

Three days later another B-29 'Bockscar', dropped a second nuclear weapon on Nagasaki. Often overlooked, it was the second mission that brought the Second World War to an end, though it nearly ended in disaster.

The decision was made to drop the second A-bomb after the Hiroshima detonation because nothing definitive was heard from the Japanese. The mission was called Special Mission No.16. The primary target was Kokura because it was Japan's principal production source for automatic weapons. The city was also home to the Mitsubishi steel and arms works, and one of the largest shipbuilding and naval centres in Japan.

On 8 August 1945, the 509th's Operation Order No.39 was given. It stated there would be three aircraft for the mission to Kokura. Major Charles W Sweeny was assigned to command *Bockscar,* the strike aircraft. The bomber would carry the atomic bomb called 'Fat Man'. The bomb would be armed and ready to drop prior to embarking on the mission, due to the complexity of its implosion system. Three officers were added to the normal crew of ten; Lt Commander Fred Ashworth, US Navy, the weaponeer in charge of the bomb; his assistant Lt Philip Barnes, and Lt Jacob Beser, radar counter-measures specialist.

The second B-29 named *Full House* was assigned to Major James I Hopkins Jr. It would carry photographic equipment and scientific personnel. Group Captain Leonard Cheshire (RAF), Winston Churchill's official representative, was also on board. Captain Fred Bock, instead of flying his normal aircraft (*Bockscar*), was to pilot *The Great Artiste*. Since this carried special electronic measuring instruments on the previous Hiroshima mission, it was decided that the aircraft would be used in the same capacity for the Kokura flight. William L Laurence, a reporter from the *New York Times*, also flew on the *Artiste*. He later won a Pulitzer Prize for his reporting.

The B-29s of the 509th were specifically modified to carry the atomic bombs. The bombers could not carry conventional bombs. All the armament was stripped out of the aircraft except for the twin 0.5-in calibre machine-guns in the tail turret, which were retained for self-defence. The removal of the armament gave the bombers a significant weight reduction and allowed an enlarged bomb-bay. The B-29 also utilised the latest fuel injection system and reversible props on their engines, which later played a vital role in the mission and the recovery of the bomber *Bockscar* to the Okinawa base.
The crews practised dropping 4,536 kg (10,000lb) 'pumpkins' on 12 Japanese targets. Each individual bomb contained 2,494 kg (5,500lb) of explosives. *Bockscar's* crew flew four missions to prepare for the A-bomb drop.

The final briefing took place in the early hours of the morning 9 August. Two B-29s were sent to the target areas one hour before the strike aircraft to report the weather conditions. *Bockscar* took off at 3.49am Tinian (local) time The weather in the area was so bad the normal rendezvous point of Iwo Jima was changed to Yaku Shima. The problem was that only two aircraft arrived, *Bockscar* and *The Great Artiste*. The third aircraft *Full House*, lost contact with the others due to poor visibility. It was agreed that Major Sweeny in *Bockscar* would stay 15 minutes at the rendezvous point, but instead he remained for 45. Because of this, the fuel situation on *Bockscar* was getting critical. The aircraft also had other problems.

With 600 gallons of fuel in the rear bomb-bay that could not be transferred to the wing tanks because of a malfunctioning fuel transfer pump. Repairing it would have taken too long, and would probably have led to postponing the mission because of changing weather conditions. After 45 minutes, Sweeney gave up and turned towards Kokura with a single B-29 escort.

Meanwhile, on *Bockscar* further problems developed. The 'black box' that armed the bomb began to flash its red light irregularly which meant something was malfunctioning. Luckily, Lt Barnes, the electronics officer discovered the problem. The wiring on two small rotary switches was crossed. Barnes quickly corrected the problem.

Upon arrival at Kokura, the area was covered by very heavy cloud, instead of the favourable conditions forecasted. The aircraft circled the city three times in different directions but visibility was terrible, so the decision was made to go to the secondary target Nagasaki. Remarkably, the bomber never encountered any enemy fighters while flying over Kokura.

Visibility at Nagasaki was not much better with similar heavy cloud cover. The aircrafts fuel problem was becoming decidedly worse, so the decision was made to drop the bomb by radar. Using radar to drop the bomb was against orders, but it was the only solution. The navigator, Van Pelt, began to use it to ensure they were over the city when suddenly the bombardier Beahan called out: "I got a hole ! I can see it ! I can see the target !" Beahan took over the bomb run, set up the Norden bombsight in the remaining 40 seconds, and bombed the target visually

After the bomb was dropped. Sweeney turned 150° away from the blast area and put the bomber in an evasive 60° bank to avoid the effects of the blast. Even though the crew wore welder goggles, a bright blue light could be seen illuminating the cabin 50 seconds after the release.

The 'mushroom' cloud looked like a boiling cauldron of oil. It was filled with a myriad of colours, but the predominant colour was salmon. The crew felt three separate shock waves, the first being the most severe. In fact all the colours of the rainbow could be seen in the mushroom cloud.

Sweeny made one wide circle over the cloud before changing course for Okinawa because they did not have enough fuel to return to Tinian. The low level fuel problem now became of great concern.

The mixture was leaned and the props were pulled to a range extending low rpm. *Bockscar* arrived at Yontan airfield, Okinawa and Sweeney tried to contact the control tower, but with no success. He ordered Lt Fred Olivi, the co-pilot to fire the flare pistol to alert the personnel at the field, but again there was no response. In desperation, Sweeney exclaimed, "I'm coming straight in !". Olivi recalled:
We came in at 140 mph, which was too fast. As we touched down, our aircraft began to swerve to the left towards a row of parked airplanes. The reversible props saved the bomber and brought it under control. As soon as we taxied off the runway the No.2 engine stopped. Starved of fuel !
Sweeney had to stand on the brakes, and make a swerving 90° turn at the end of the runway to avoid going over the cliff and into the sea. There was an estimated seven gallons (26 litres) of fuel left in the bomber's tanks. In all, the exhausted crew endured a gruelling 10.5 hour mission from take-off at Tinian to landing at Okinawa.

In the mess hall, while the bomber was being refuelled, while the crew were getting their food, a cook on the servery told the crew that he had heard the war was going to end because a single Lockheed P-38 Lightning fighter had dropped a bomb the size of a golf ball on Japan ! Obviously the crew could not respond because they still had to remain silent about the Special Mission.

While at the Okinawa base, Sweeney and Ashworth borrowed a jeep and went to the base communications building to send a report to Tinian. However, it could not be sent without permission of the commanding officer, General Jimmy Dolittle, who had recently be sent to Okinawa to oversee the arrival of the US 8th Air Force units from Europe and to prepare them for future operations in the Pacific. Dolittle listened intently as both men explained what happened. Both men were nervous about telling the story to the General because they believed the weapon had not hit the target directly. While they spoke, Dolittle pulled out a map and the men pointed to where they thought 'Fat Man' had exploded. Fortunately, it detonated over an industrial section of the city and not in the densely populated area. Dolittle gave the airmen solace by saying: "I'm sure General Spaatz will be much happier that the bomb went off in the river valley rather than the city, with the resulting much lower casualties." He quickly authorised the communications section to send Sweeny's coded after-action report.

The mission was a success and it changed history. The bomb killed 35,000 and injured 60,000, but it prompted the Japanese surrender. Major Charles W Sweeny was awarded the Silver Star for the mission, and the rest of the crew including navigator Captain James F Van Pelt Jr. and co-pilot Lt J Olivi, received the Distinguished Flying Cross.

When the Japanese surrender came following Special Mission No.16 on 14 August 1945, no fewer than 828 B-29 Superfortresses were airborne on conventional bombing missions. During the Pacific War, the 20th Air Force's B-29s dropped 169,676 tons of bombs, of which 105,486 tons were incendiary and the remainder high explosive (HE), and laid a large but unknown quantity of mines. 414 B-29s were lost on combat missions and 105 more destroyed or scrapped after incidents or accidents involving non-operational activities. Another ten B-29s were lost en-route from America to combat theatres in the Pacific. By VJ Day the 20th Air Force had some 1,100 B-29s on inventory, including about 50 F-13 reconnaissance variants.

In its original bomber role, in 1946, the B-29 became the mainstay of the newly formed Strategic Air Command for a while and during the Korean War of 1950-53, by which time it was gradually being withdrawn, although it was almost in daily operation. In the three year conflict B-29s dropped 167,100 tons of bombs in 21,000 sorties, shot down 33 enemy aircraft including 16 Mikoyan MiG-15s and destroyed or probably destroyed a further 28 MiGs. Total B-29 losses were 34, of which only 20 were due to enemy action.

From early 1948 there followed two years of skirmishes on the border between the Democratic People's Republic of Korea in the North and the Republic of Korea in the South. The latter pro-west, and the former aligning itself with the Soviet Union and its Communist allies.
Bomber Wings of B-29s were deployed by Strategic Air Command to Korea in 1950, and were primarily used against troop and tank concentrations and supply dumps until August. After that the B-29s began to strike industrial centres and communication links in the North, in support of the Allied invasion at Inchon.

Intense FEAF Bomber Command missions commenced on 9 September 1950, with B-29 operations against railheads and marshalling yards, in support of the impending Inchon landings to push communist North Koreans forces from South Korea. Two months later, on 23 November the FEAF began a major offensive to support the push by the Eighth Army against communist forces in North Korea.
The following year from early January through to mid-April, B-29 Superfortresses dropped massive 12,000lb Tarzon bombs on important transportation routes including roads, bridges and railways, disrupting the North Korean army's supply lines. By 14 April, B-29s had destroyed 48 out of 60 bridges and 27 out of 39 marshalling yards — strategic targets assigned to them in North Korea — at a cost of eight bombers destroyed.

On 25 August 1951, 35 B-29s, escorted by 23 F9F Panthers and F2H Banshees from USS *Essex* dropped 291 tons of bombs on Rashin, close to the Siberian border, severely damaging the towns marshalling yards. On 23 October, the biggest air battle of the war to date, involved ten B-29 bombers escorted by 89 fighters (mostly North American F-86 Sabres) that were intercepted by about 150 MiG-15s while attacking Namsi, south of the Yula River. Three bombers were shot down and four made emergency landings in South Korea, while six MiGs were destroyed.

The following day a daylight raid was made against a road/rail bridge at Sunchon by B-29s — one bomber was lost. Final daylight raids were made on 27/28 October against road/rail bridges, without loss. Intense aerial combat continued throughout the remainder of the year the FEAF inflicting high losses on the communist MiGs. Full-scale use was made of air-to-air (AAR) refuelling to support ground attack missions and the KB-29M tankers supported Republic F-84E Thunderjet fighter-bomber operations.

(Authors Note: B-29A 'Enola Gay' can be seen at the Air and Space Museum on Independence Avenue in Washington DC 20560, USA). Colonel Paul W. Tibbetts, who flew the raid, named the famous Superfortress after his mother. B-29 Bockscar is displayed inside the USAF Museum at Dayton, Ohio.

In 1953, Kadena-based B-29s, escorted by Osan-based F-86s continued their bombing of the North. Through until July, North Korea airfields came under heavy attack, while North American F-86Fs, supported UN ground forces to stabilise the front-line prior to an all-out strike against enemy troops on 13 July. Within six days North Korea agreed an Armistice, and after the terms had been accepted by South Korea's President Rhee, this was signed on 27 July. Ninety-two B-29s were converted to flying tankers with a single large fuel tank filling each bomb-bay, transfer pumps and a hose that could be unreeled and secured to the receiver aircraft. Seventy-four B-29 bombers were modified to facilitate AAR, with one bomb-bay modified to receive fuel by this method. Later, 116 B-29s were modified at Renton as KB-29P 'flying boom' tankers to overcome the drawbacks that had become apparent with the KB-29Ms. The flying boom method permitting a direct mechanical connection between the aircraft and much higher fuel transfer rates.

In 1944, Pratt & Whitney converted a B-29A to have 3,500hp R-4360 Wasp Major engines, and this became known as the XB-44. To give rise to 200 examples of an improved B-29 with a larger fin, more powerful engines, new undercarriage and other refinements, the B-29D was ordered in July 1945, and production was entrusted to Boeing's Renton plant. After VJ Day the order was cut to 60 and the new Superfort redesignated B-50 with the Boeing Model number 345-2. It was in fact a 75 per cent new airplane, with a new aluminium wing structure some 16 per cent stronger and 26 per cent more efficient than that of its illustrious ancestor, while weighing some 294 kg (650lb) less. The B-50 gave the USAF Strategic Air Command a true nuclear capability.

First flight of the B-50 took place on 25 June 1947 and, apart from the engine installation, the principle external change was in the increase of about five feet in the height of the vertical tail surfaces, which, to permit stowage in standard hangars, could be folded down. Less evident new features were a stronger and lighter wing structure, stronger and faster-retracting undercarriage, hydraulic rudder boost and nose-wheel steering, and, instead of the conventional rubber de-icer boots, it had a hot-air anti-icing system which kept the leading edges of the wing and tail free of ice at all times.

Altogether, 371 B-50 series aircraft were built, 80 B-50A ; 45 of the generally similar B-50B; 222 B-50D (Boeing Model number 345-9-6) aircraft with a new top front barbette, one piece Plexiglass nose cone, and provision for flying boom flight refuelling and under-wing auxiliary fuel tanks ; and, finally, 27 TB-50F unarmed bombing and navigational trainers.

From 1947, many of the earlier versions of the B-50 Stratoforts were converted to serve with SAC's strategic reconnaissance squadrons, carrying cameras and electronic search equipment. Other conversion - and sometimes, re-conversion - programmes produced such variants as TB-50 crew trainers, WB-50s for weather reconnaissance, and, finally, 136 KB-50 triple-hose refuelling tankers for Tactical Air Command, each with two 5,200lb static thrust General Electric J47 under-wing turbojets in addition to their normal powerplant.

For those wishing to see the big Boeing B-29A Superfortress serial *44-62070/N529B* 'Fifi', a visit to the Confederate Air Force (CAF) museum and support facilities at Midland-Odessa Airport, Texas is well worthwhile. *Fifi* was one of 35 B-29s found on a weapons range in California in the mid-1960s. The best of the bunch, '*070*', was made airworthy and flown out in 1971. Only one flight was sanctioned by the USAF intense negotiations followed to allow further flights after restoration. Fifi remains the world's only airworthy B-29. Prior to its restoration by the CAF, *'Fifi'* had been used as a US naval gunnery target.

Chapter 2   Boeing B.47 Stratojet

Overshadowed by its bigger stable-mate, the B-52 Stratofortress, the B.47 Stratojet has been largely overlooked in the annals of aviation history. Although the two aircraft were similar in configuration and design, in reality both bombers were originally developed to fulfil different mission requirements. Work on the XB-47 prototype, started in 1943, when jet propulsion was still in its infancy. The original requirement was for a fast photo reconnaissance aircraft and a medium-bomber. Initial designs featured a straight-wing with jet engines added, but it was soon realised this design would not provide sufficient lift or performance. Subsequent studies of WW II captured German research papers on swept-wing designs, confirmed earlier findings of work carried out by NACA and the engineers opted for a thin swept-wing design for their new jet-bomber. Two prototype Boeing XB-47s were ordered in 1946, featuring a 35° swept-wing with six pod-mounted GE engines —two twin-unit and two single unit nacelles under each wing. Cockpit configuration more resembled a fighter than a bomber with the pilot and co-pilot sitting under a single bubble canopy, with the third crew member, the bombardier/ navigator, sitting behind the transparent nose. Initially no crew ejection seats were fitted, although these were fitted later as part of the modification programmes.

The USAF ordered two XB-47 prototypes in the spring of 1946, and the first, serial 46-065 of the revolutionary new bombers was rolled out at Boeing's Renton plant on 12 September 1947, having its maiden flight on 17 December 1947 fitted with six Allison J35 turbojets. The aircraft flown by Boeing test pilots Robert M Robbins and Scott Oster taking off from Boeing Field, Seattle, and landing at Moses Lake AFB, Washington. Between 8-15 August a number of USAF test pilots flew the aircraft for some eighty-three hours compiling flight reports that made it clear that more refinements were needed. Most important, the tests revealed the bomber was sorely underpowered. To remedy the lack of power, the second prototype, serial 46-066, was fitted with six 5,200lb s. t. General Electric J47-GE-3 engines (retrofitted to the first prototype in October 1949), and when 46-066 made its maiden flight on 21 July 1948 it became immediately apparent that the new engines could provide sufficient output to meet the performance needed to meet the exacting USAF specification.

On 28 October 1948, the Air Force placed an order for ten B-47As, with a commitment for three more B-47As (which was later cancelled) and 41 B-47Bs (the first series production model), these the first of an eventual total of 2,042 Stratojets built. The aircraft to become SAC's primary medium bomber until replaced by the General Dynamics FB-111 Aardvark and was the first in a long line of successful turbo-jet-powered military aircraft produced by Boeing including, the Model B.707/C-135/KC-135 and the B-52 Stratofortress.

By June 1949, the production order for B-47Bs had been increased to 102 (later cut back to 87) on the basis of the mainly successful flight trials flown by the ten B-47As.

Boeing equipped the series B-47Bs with six J47-GE-11 turbojet engines and strengthened the airframe to permit take-off weights in excess of 200,000lb. An in-flight nose-mounted refuelling receptacle was added to increase the bombers operational range and a Nesa glass windshield eliminated the earlier wind shield wiper arrangement to keep it clear for the pilot.

The rear gun fire-control radar was upgraded to the B-4 system and the bomber was equipped with the K-4A bombing navigation system, AN/APS-54 warning radar, AN/APT-5A electronics counter-measures (ECM) system, and a standard capacity 18,000lb bomb-bay, which could be increased to a maximum combat bomb-load of 22,000lb (providing the ability to carry a large yield thermonuclear weapon).

A novel feature was the 18 internally mounted solid propellant rockets to provide ATO — assisted take-off — for aircraft with full payloads. With early jet engines being rather low on power, the extra 18,000lbs of thrust was essential. The first prototype used Allison J35-A-2 engines each developing only 2,750lb of thrust with the second prototype using the uprated General Electric J47-GE-3s rated at 5,200lbs. As the B-47 and its engines evolved, the engines increased in power with the most prolific B-47E being fitted with J47-GE-25/25A of 7,200lbs thrust with water injection.

However, initial B-47Es retained ATO fitment although later variants had a belly-mounted jettisonable rack of thirty-three rockets. Even so, a number of early aircraft were lost on take-off as a result of engine failure, especially if the failed engine was an outboard one.

The aircraft presented landing difficulties for pilots, requiring a landing run twice that of the B-29. This was overcome by fitment of a 9.7 metre (32ft) diameter ribbon type drag parachute. The aircraft had an impressive bomb-load of 4,500kg (10,000lb) or in special circumstances a single 10,000kg (22,000lb) bomb could be carried. Originally intended to carry a free-fall nuclear device the crews practiced low-level 'lob-bombing' techniques which unfortunately resulted in a number of over-stressed airframes, requiring an extensive airframe strengthening modification programme in 1958, code-named Project *Milk Bottle*.

After the North Koreans Peoples Republic invaded South Korea on 25 June, 1950, the demand for Stratojets began to outstrip Boeing's production capacity. To ease production backlogs Boeing sub-contracted two more Stratojet production facilities to Lockheed Aircraft at Marietta, Georgia and Douglas Aircraft at Tulsa, Oklahoma.
As with all complex military equipment and aircraft, inevitably changes were required. The Air Force and SAC listed over 2,000 changes to enable the bomber to deploy nuclear weapons. With the Cold War deepening, the USAF increased its Stratojet order of B-47Bs to 1,760 (a mix of B/RB-47s). However, the B model series production run ended at 397, primarily because of the decision to produce the much improved B-47E.

Flight experience with the B-47B made its successor, the B-47E, an outstanding bomber. SAC equipped 27 Strategic Air Command medium bomber wings (with four bomb squadrons, each with 15 aircraft).
The bomber soon became an important element in United States nuclear deterrence and foreign policy. On 12 January 1954, Secretary of State John Foster Dulles declared the United States would rely on 'massive nuclear retaliation' to counter a conventional or nuclear attack against Europe or nuclear strike against the North American continent.

With the aircraft fitted with a starboard boom flight refuelling receptacle and the 'E' variant fitted with 1,500 gallon auxiliary fuel tanks beneath the wings the Strategic Air Command (SAC) crews often found themselves deployed on long-range training flights world-wide. The bomber carried a three-man crew in a tandem arranged cockpit with the co-pilot responsible for the two 0.50in calibre tail guns on the A & B models and the two 20mm cannons on the E model. The third crew member the bombardier/navigator was seated in the lower fuselage, ejecting downwards in an emergency.

The first ten B-47As were essentially development aircraft. During the test programme the XB-47 gave an indication of its potential when it flew 2,289 miles across America in 3 hours 46 minutes. Due in the main to the advanced nature of the design and initial manufacturing problems, B-47 Stratojets did not appear in large numbers until 1952. Ten B-47As fitted with J47-GE-11 engines appeared in 1950 entering service with the 306th Bomb Wing (BW) in 1951, at MacDill AFB, Florida, for training purposes.

Eventually the B-47 became the back-bone of SAC and the most numerous bomber of the nuclear age. Nothing before or since was ever quite like it. At the peak of its strength SAC had more than 1,700 B-47 Stratojets in service at the same time and had hundreds of them in the air — some on nuclear alert — at once. In total, an amazing, 2,289 Stratojets had been constructed when production ceased, of which most were bombers.

The first operational aircraft for the USAF being the first of 399 B-47Bs (serial 50-0008) with 5,800lb s. t. J-47-GE-23 engines handed over to Colonel Michael McCoy, commander of the 306th Bomb Wing on 23 October 1951. The last B-47B rolled of the production line in June 1953. Although, at this time the USAF were still not happy with the airplane and funded two modification programmes, *Ebb Tide* and *High Noon* which again included fitment of uprated engines (6,000lb s. t. J47-GE-25). Most B models were subsequently modified to E standard and 51 were converted to crew trainers designated TB-47B, to transition SAC crews onto the E model. The problem of poor range on the B model was addressed by fitment of enormous auxiliary fuel tanks, with a combined capacity of 3,560 U.S. gallons, under each wing. Provision was also made for in-flight refuelling.

The most prolific variant was the B-47E of which 1,350 were built (Boeing 691, Douglas 274 and Lockheed 385), entering service in 1953. Extra thrust brought the top speed to around 650 mph, with other internal refinements including an improved radar and heavier calibre tail guns. Later, a number of B-47E became B-47E-II when given stronger wings for low-altitude operations. Aircraft designed for the photo-reconnaissance role were designated RB-47E or RB-47H and there were some RB-47Ks. These airplanes were devoid of offensive armament, carrying up to eleven cameras instead. The 'H' variant was primarily intended for location of enemy surface radar sites and carried a crew of two pilots and an observer, and with the carriage of special equipment it could carry an additional three crew members in a modified bomb-bay capsule.

Some series aircraft were built by Douglas at Tulsa, and some by Lockheed at Marietta, although the majority were built by Boeing at Wichita and Seattle. In the nine years between 1947 and 1957 some 2,048 aircraft were series-produced by these three companies.

In 1956, after nuclear sabre-rattling by the Soviets forced Britain, France, and Israel to cease their Suez operations, SAC flexed its Stratojet power. More than 1,000 B-47s and Boeing KC-97 Stratotankers conducted a simulated 8,000 mile combat mission over North America and the Arctic — well within radar detection range of Soviet long-range radars. While one aircraft, a B-47E, from Wright Field, Air Development Center, in an endurance demonstration, remained airborne for three days, eight hours, 36 minutes, travelling a distance of 39,000 miles - supported by numerous in-flight refuellings.

In 1957 SAC had over 1,200 B-47's in service equipping eighty-one operational squadrons, the type giving more than ten years excellent service until being phased out of the front-line inventory in 1963. Two hundred and forty-eight aircraft were built for the photo-reconnaissance role (RB-47E) and 32 for the electronic reconnaissance role (ERB/RB-47H) and a number were used as special test-beds. Thirty-four B-47Es were converted to WB-47E variants for weather reconnaissance duties. As were a further ten as ERB/RB-47H training aircraft.

With its swept-back wings, six jet engines under-slung in pods and sleek, slim fuselage, the B-47 Stratojet was of great concern to Moscow. The E model could carry 9,072kg (20,000lb) of bombs on a long-range mission, or alternatively a Mk 43 Atomic bomb could be carried or four Mk 57 free-fall bombs each generating a yield of 20-50 kilotons. It is not surprising therefore, at a military air show in Washington in the 1950s — at Bolling AFB, DC — three Soviet military visitors looked on in awe as a B-47E demonstrated the latest 'toss-bombing' technique that came into use by SAC at that time.

The B-47 bomber had the 'feel' — and sometimes acted — like a fighter. Pilot and co-pilot sat in tandem beneath a long, slender bubble canopy, with the bombardier placed in the nose. The crew normally breathing oxygen from the moment they 'strapped in' on the ground. Their accommodation was comfortable but far from luxurious, and really not ideal for an long-range air-to-air refuelled mission lasting many hours: there was only a narrow catwalk to provide some relief from the confines of the ejection seat — itself not considered very reliable.

On a typical mission, an auxiliary power unit was used to fire up the B-47 and a ground crewman used hand signals to communicate with the pilot to guide him out of his parking spot, on the hard standing. The aircraft had tandem 'bicycle' landing gear with outrigger wheels to support the wing-tips (alias the Lockheed U-2 Spyplane) and this made the bomber to appear it was shooting skyward whilst still on the ground. In fact, the aircraft was not easy to taxi because of its high angle of attach.

Jet-assisted take-off (JATO) bottles were 'slung' on the aft fuselage of the B-47 to give the heavily laden bombers extra thrust to get into the air. With a full bomb-load, the Stratojet at a maximum overload weight of 220,000lb was far from adequately powered and it was often arranged for the bomber to take-off with a reduced fuel state to be 'topped off' when airborne and into the mission.

Throughout most of its operational career the B-47 was refuelled by the piston-engined Boeing KC-97 tankers, and it was necessary for the pilot to throttle his jet engines back and remain close to the stall in Soviet fighters of the era had been designed to intercept prop-driven bombers like the Convair B-36 and Boeing B-50 — which remained a vital part of SAC's striking force at this time. The maximum speed of the B-47 was almost equal to that of a Mikoyan MiG-15 or MiG-17 fighter, so that neither of these early Soviet jet fighters could realistically expect to intercept it. In 1954, one RB-47E eluded attacking Soviet MiG-17s by entering Finland's airspace, whereby Finland filed diplomatic complaints with the US State Department concerning the violation of its sovereign airspace (allegations denied by US Air Force Europe officials in Germany).

Although slower that the supersonic MiG-19 and MiG-21 which entered service after the bomber did, the B-47 was nevertheless fast enough that it was unlikely that even these aircraft would be able to prevent its penetration into Soviet airspace.

So although the Stratojet had a gun unit (two 20mm guns on the B-47E, these operated by the co-pilot), it was very likely it would never be attacked from the rear. On the one occasion a RB-47 reconnaissance plane was shot down, over the Barents Sea on 1 July 1960, it was because the crew believed that the Soviets merely wished to escort them. In the 1950s, the Soviets also lacked an adequate surface-to-air (SAM) system, so that a typical B-47 mission was flown at high altitude, where jet engine fuel consumption was optimum.

A typical mission, flown from Kadena AB, Okinawa, - not yet returned to Japan in the 1950s - against the strategic bomber base at Andyr in the Soviet Eastern District meant a round trip of 6,000 miles over a duration of eleven hours with two in-flight refuellings by Boeing KC-97 tankers. The mission usually a simple lo-hi-lo profile, with the B-47 simply climbing to optimum altitude of around 32,000ft and proceeding more or less directly to the target area. No evasive action was deemed necessary.

The B-47 Stratojet set numerous speed and distance records during this period of operational service. Typical was a June 1954 deployment in which three Stratojets of the 22nd Bomb Wing, led by Major General Walter C Sweeney Jr. Commander of the US 15th Air Force, completed a non-stop 6,700-mile flight from March AFB, California to Yokota AB, Japan, in 14 hours 51 minutes with two in-flight refuellings.

In the Korean War (1950-53), the only SAC bombers committed to action were the Boeing B-29 Superfortresses. Through the 1950s, the SAC force changed its long-range strategic bomber equipment from a nearly all-prop inventory of Convair B-36 and Boeing B-50 aircraft to an nearly all-jet fleet of Boeing B-47s and B-52s, and at the end of the decade, the remarkable Convair B-58 Hustler began to enter service. At this time the USAF SAC bombers were the only deterrent to Soviet ambitions, there being no Intercontinental Ballistic Missiles (ICBMs), neither on land or aboard submarines.

While the USAF adapted its post-WW II bomber fleet well to meet its long-range strategic requirements when joined in the 1950s by the B-52 Stratofortress and B-58 Hustler, other benefits accrued from the significant advances in bomber aircraft technology of the post-war period. While nuclear weapons were being improved, particularly by way of their size so light-bombers and tactical fighters could carry them, so, too, were jet aircraft designs, being made ever better. For a period, the USAF operated several light-bombers. — not part of SAC, but very much part of America's world-wide commitment and, when stationed near, Soviet borders, regarded as a threat.

The Glenn L Martin Company, produced a unique three-engined design, the XB-51, which incorporated a variable incidence, sweptback, drooped wing, a T-tail and tandem main-wheels. With its sleek fighter-like design and capable of 1,048 km/h (651 mph), the XB-51 also introduced a feature unique to the Martin Company — a rotary, internal bomb-bay which enabled the aircraft to drop bombs while flying at high-speed.

First flown on 28 October 1949 and tested extensively into the mid-1950s, the XB-51 had three 2,340 kg (5,200lb) s .t. General Electric J47 engines, two in pylons on the lower forward sides of the fuselage, and the third located internally in the rear fuselage at the base of the tail. Landing gear consisted of two pairs of large wheels mounted in tandem or bicycle style, retracting into the fuselage. Choice of this type of gear permitted the use of an extremely thin, high-speed swept-wing section, no storage space needed for the retracted wheels being required in the wing.

With a crew only of two, pilot and radio operator, the XB-51 was nearly as much like a fighter as a bomber. One of the two prototypes appeared briefly in SAC livery, but this was little more than a hopeful gesture on Glenn L Martin's part.

Major Charles E Yeager once flew five 'realistic' bombing missions in the XB-51 in less than three hours, while Martin pilots Pat Tibbs and Russ Schleeh reported that virtually every aspect of the bomber, from its MiG-like T-tail to the eight 20-mm nose guns, worked perfectly. The bomber could carry two tons of bombs and 1,300 cannon rounds over a combat radius of 500 miles
.

However, in a head-to-head evaluation against the British EE Canberra, the North American B-45 Tornado and even the North American Savage soon showed up the severe shortcomings of the futuristic looking Martin XB-51. Extremely un-manoeuvrable, a poor bombing platform, with poor short field performance, all the XB-51 had to offer was speed, and it wasn't much faster than the Canberra, even at high level. In an evaluation fly-off, the tight-turning Canberra demonstrated all of the required manoeuvres over the airfield with time to spare for an impressive air display in front the evaluation panel, and a short landing. The XB-51 only managed two long straight passes over the runway within the same time limit.

A variety of aircraft were evaluated for the nuclear bombing role, including almost every jet fighter in the US inventory. Among these, the Republic F-84E and F-84G Thunderjet, the F-84F Thunderstreak and the RF-84F and RF-84K Thunderflash were operated by SAC squadrons, the RF-84K being carried in the bomb-bay of a massive Convair B-36 Peacemaker bomber. Various commands did have fighters in the nuclear weapon delivery role. Even the Air National Guard were so equipped. Tactical Fighter Squadrons equipped with F-84F Thunderstreaks flew with nuclear 'shapes' and practised nuclear delivery methods. Some of these units actually re-assigned to Tactical Air Command (TAC) and deployed to Europe during the Berlin crisis, to back-up in-theatre nuclear strike forces which included North American F-86 Sabres, F-100 Super Sabres and McDonnell F-101 Voodoos.

The 81st Tactical Fighter Wing at RAF Bentwaters, and Woodbridge in the UK, operated McDonnell F-101A and F-101C Voodoo described by a pilot as "absolutely useless for any job except carrying an atomic bomb under the centre-line station".

Somewhere between the two extremes - the US Navy's batman sized Douglas A-4D Skyhawk, which was the smallest warplane ever to carry a nuclear bomb and SAC's massive B-36, the largest - lay the extraordinarily successful Canberra light-bomber developed by English Electric in the UK and used by numerous air forces throughout the world in several confrontations. First flown in 1949 in the UK, as the highly modified Martin B-57 (virtually a different airplane, after modification), it subsequently gave good service in Vietnam, albeit suffering a high attrition rate, after being the first foreign design accepted for front-line service with the USAF.

Glenn L Martin in Baltimore, unsuccessful with its own XB-51 licence-built the EE Canberra as the B-57 'Canberra' and the aircraft served with distinction. The typical series B-57B was powered by two 7,200lb thrust Wright J65-W-5 turbojets Sapphire engines also a licence-built British design. With a maximum speed of 582 mph, the B-57B was armed with eight forward-firing .50in machine-guns and could carry 6,000lb of bombs plus 16 under-wing rockets over a typical radius of 500 miles. Martin's B-57B used tandem cockpit seating rather than the side-by-side arrangement found on the British aircraft at the time.

The type was never used by SAC, but communist nations clearly viewed nuclear-capable B-57s on their borders as a strategic threat. B-57s carrying nuclear weapons were deployed on 24-hour alert at bases in France and at Clark AFB, in the Philippines during the late 1960s, before the B-57 force became totally committed to the war in South-east Asia. These aircraft were part of Tactical Air Command inventory, but practised nuclear delivery procedures, and would have been sent on deep interdiction missions against targets in the USSR whose importance was at least semi-strategic.

Meanwhile, while the SAC force continued its transition from B-36 to B-52 and from B-47 to B-58, the development of light bombers continued with an air force design based on the US Navy's Douglas A3D Skywarrior - the Douglas B-66 Destroyer. The twin-engine, swept-wing B-66 made its first flight on 28 June 1954.

Outwardly similar to the Skywarrior, the B-66 had wholly different interior systems, powerplant, and crew arrangement. First delivered as the RB-66A reconnaissance plane and powered by two 10,200lb s. t. Allison J71-A-13 turbojets, the B-66 could fly at 631 mph armed with two 20mm cannon in the tail and carrying up to 8,000lb of bombs. The only dedicated bomber version was the B-66B (72 built), which reached Tactical Air Command on 1 February 1956.

The B-66B bomber aircraft was equipped with the first all-solid state (i.e. without thermionic valves) bombing and navigation avionics equipment installed successfully in a production warplane, this being the K-5 bombing system. Later some 13 were modified to B-66E standard with improved equipment, with several electronic warfare (EW) variants produced as conversions.

In 1955, Strategic Air Command had on strength some 1,700 bombers which included 1,400 Boeing B-47 Stratojets and 300 Convair B-36 Peacemakers. This in itself, was an impressive force, but it grew still larger. In 1959, the force reached its maximum size ever, with 2,100 bombers on strength. The B-36 left service the previous year and this all-time maximum force comprised nearly all B-47s, some 1,800 of them, although SAC had also begun to operate the newer Boeing B-52 Stratofortress.

By 1960, SAC generals believed the Stratojet was nearing the end of its operational life, and should be replaced by the B-52. However, the Soviet, American nuclear brinkmanship triggered by the Cuban Missile crisis, meant the operational life of the Stratojet was extended. The last production B-47E, air-craft serial 53-6244, was delivered to SAC's 100th Bombardment Wing, Pease AFB, New Hampshire on 19 February 1957. Older Stratojets had already retired to the Air Force aircraft storage facility at Davis-Monthan AFB, Arizona. This was a gradual disposal programme, taking nine years to complete.

Colonel Paul Tibbets, the pilot of the Boeing B-29 Superfortress which dropped the Hiroshima atomic bomb waves from the cabin before taking off for the target.

Boeing B-29 *Enola Gay* 'Little Boy' on display in the Paul E. Garber facility in 1990

The two nuclear bombs dropped on Japan in 1945, Little Boy'
above, and 'Fat Man' on its transporter and wired up before
the drop from *Bocks Car*

American warplanes fill the limited parking space at the airfield known as "Fred" on Eniwetok Atoll during Operation *Redwing* in April 1956. The Stratofortress left centre is the JB-52B serial 52-0004 assigned to the effects of hydrogen bomb detonations on the airframe. Also visible are B-47s, B-50s, Douglas C-54s, SA-16 and H-19 helicopter. Some were to support *Redwing*; others were intended to gather nuclear samples

Fifi, owned by the Confederate Air Force is seen during a display at Midland, Texas in 1993, is the only airworthy B-29 Superfortress in the world. She caused a diplomatic incident a number of years earlier when she carried out a simulated blast at a Confederate Air Force Air Show to the embarrassment of the Japanese ambassador present.

Boeing B-52D Stratofortress serial 56-0591 *Tommy's Tigator*, was the only B-52 sent to the Pacific during Operation Hardtack tests in 1958, which did not include any air-dropped atomic blasts. This B-52D was subjected to overpressures during Hardtack detonation and later, in July 1959, crashed in Oregon killing a Boeing crew

The crew of the RB-52B Stratofortress serial 52-0004 The Tender Trap—Gilmore, Lewis, Anderson, Deatrick, Williams, Collins, at Eniwetok Atoll during thermo-nuclear bomb testing in April 1956.

An early model B-52 resplendent in early Strategic Air Command markings—white anti-flash underbody with all-over silver finish—the crew preparing to embark on another long-rang airborne 'alert' mission

Boeing B-52's still carry a sting in the tail, in the form of its four 0.50 calibre cannon its fire-control system, using either radar-tracking or closed-circuit television.

To undertake the low-level penetration role effectively in all weathers the B-52 force was fitted with the characteristic blisters for the Electro-optical viewing system. This consists of low-level TV and FLIR.

Mk 82 500lb free-fall bombs fitted to a triple-ejector rack

An B-52H equipped with two SRAM (short Range Attack Missile) a nuclear weapon for defence suppression during the mission

The USAF placed nearly £100,000,000 worth of orders for eight-jet Boeing B-52 Stratofortress long-range strategic-bombers to replace it's B-36 fleet. Here XB-52 serial 9231 with it's unique 'glass-house' cockpit is on an early test flight. The aircraft utilised the same type of thin 'flexible' wing and 'podded' engines as it's smaller predecessor, the Boeing B-47 Stratojet

April 1952, and the historic Boeing YB-52 prototype serial 49-231 lands, after an early test flight

B-52G of the 2nd Bombardment Wing undergoing routine maintenance on the flight-line before embarking on another long-range conventional bombing mission. A KC-10A Extender in-flight refuelling tanker can also be seen on the flight line to the rear.

The pilot and co-pilot sit side-by-side on the B-52's flight deck. At night or in bad weather, the crew can operate the bomber by referring to the prominent display screens that serve the Electro-optical Viewing System.

B-52H airplanes at Castle AFB, California, await their next training mission. Note 'iron' bombs denoting twenty operational missions.

A B-36 Peacemaker takes off assisted by the four podded turbojets mounted under-wing. "Six turning, four burning"

SAC Convair B-36J being bombed-up for another long-range Cold War mission

B-36D serial 44-92042 of the Carswell-based 7th Bomb Group, this Peacemaker went 'off-roading' for about half a mile crossing a main road before coming to rest close to the south-western perimeter of A&AEE Boscombe Down airfield in the UK.

The first production Boeing B-47A Stratojet which flew on 25 June 1950

An early model B-47 on SAC alert duties, aircraft in it's early nuclear anti-flash white colour scheme

Early model B-47 on SAC alert duties. All ground movements were made under the directions of the ground-crew marshal—there was no other means of communication with the ground handlers on the ground at this time.

SAC Convair B-58 Hustler nuclear bombers were refuelled in flight by piston-engined Boeing KC-97 tankers effectively developed Boeing B-29 Stratofortresses

The Convair B-58 Hustler, the world's first production Mach 2.0 strategic nuclear bomber.

The sleek fighter-like Convair B-58 Hustler demanded great respect from its crews and ground maintenance personnel. It presented many problems although engine changes were relatively straightforward.

The restored Northrop N9MB Flying Wing—can be seen at the Planes of Fame Air Museum, Chino Airport, California. With a 18.3 metres (60ft) span, the restoration was undertaken by volunteers led by Douglas Aircraft engineer Ron Hackworth

The unique Northrop N9MB Flying Wing—John Northrop's first step into designing a flying wing tailless strategic bomber

The Northrop XB-35 was an impressive airplane, and its size is indicated by the accompanying WWII Lockheed P-62 night-fighter chase plane.

Northrop converted two XB-35s for jet propulsion. With either 4,000lb s.t. Allison J45-A-5 engines. First conversion flew in October 1947

Preceding the YB-49 jet was the series Northrup B-35 of which fourteen were built. The graceful airplane proved a large flying-wing was practical but the USAF was not prepared to take such a radical step at this time of putting them into front-line service

The General Dynamics FB-111A strategic bomber, based on the F-111D fighter-bomber design, made its maiden flight on 30 July 1967. It has a variable geometry wing and is powered by two 20,350lb s.t. Pratt & Whitney TF30-P-7 turbofan engines. Somewhat larger than the F-111D length is 73ft 6 ins and wing-span 33ft 11in. MToW is 119.00lb

One of the sixty GD FB-111A operated by Strategic Air Command (SAC) - armed and ready to go in its hardened shelter.

An impressive array of finned conventional bombs loaded on the FB-111A Ardvark's starboard under-wing racks. A similar array would be carried on the port installation

Rockwell B-1B Lancer fresh off the production line, awaiting transfer to the paint shop

Deveopment B-1B at Edwards AFB, California awaiting clearance for take-off

Rockwell B-1B Lancer parked alongside its B-52 big brother at a USAF 'Eagle Meet' in the UK at RAF Mildenhall near Newmarket, Suffolk in the East of England

'Stealth' technology, or low radar observability, played a large part in the B-1B's development, and it exhibits a very small radar cross section with its sleek design and the front-on profile

A B-1B Lancer receiving attention on a hot summer's day at RAF Fairford in Gloucestershire at UK IAT Open Day

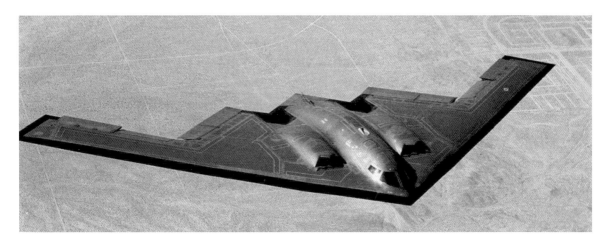

The distinct shape of B-2 Spirit serial 80329 over the California desert during flight trials

An B-2 Spirit en-route Baghdad during Operation *Enduring Freedom* about to take on fuel from an orbiting KC-10A Extender tanker.

Chapter 3 B-52 Stratofortress

In mid-1952, flight-testing began of an aircraft that was to become a legend in the annals of bomber aircraft history, even though it remains a major component of the USAF's 21st century battle order, more than fifty years later. The Boeing B-52, made its inaugural flight on 15 April 1952. The design of the massive swept-wing eight-engined bomber enveloped all the advanced aeronautical technology and standards available immediately post-WW II when Boeing started work on the project in 1948-49, all aimed at giving the newly-formed United States Air Force (USAF) and its Strategic Air Command the very best it could provide for a very long-range strategic bomber to deliver nuclear weapons.

Today (2006), the Boeing B-52 remains one vital element of the manned bomber inventory fielded by SAC's successor, Air Combat Command. Now, using the latest munitions, including precision-guided weapons and cruise missiles, allied to the latest state-of-the–art avionics, that were just science fiction when the prototype, tandem-crewed XB-52 serial 49-230, took off on that spring day more than half a century ago.

The B-52 Stratofortress was the first jet bomber which could fly missions to any part of the globe. When the aircraft first appeared in 1952 it was taken for granted that new bombers would appear every few months. The Boeing B-52 was in fact, bigger and more powerful than most, but it is doubtful that anyone who watched the roll-out of the prototype would have believed that today in 2006, the type is not only still is service but will remain in the front-line for at least another thirty years. There is absolutely no replacement. The Rockwell B-1 Lancer designed to replace it, instead, operating alongside it in Air Combat Commands 21st century inventory. This, a situation neither the Air Force in Washington nor Boeing in Seattle ever dreamed of when the project that became the B-52 began in 1945.

At that time all heavy bombers had piston engines. Jet engines were only acceptable for fighters, and even then they reduced range and endurance rather seriously so that early jet fighters — in Korea, for example — were extremely limited in the missions they could fly, particularly at low level. Jet bombers were very hard to justify, because though they had superior performance they could not even fly to their targets unaided, let alone fly there and back.

When Boeing and Convair battled for the proposed new strategic heavy bomber to replace the B-36 — before the latter had ever flown — they never seriously looked at jets at all. There seemed to be two choices. One was the massive Pratt & Whitney R-4360 Wasp Major piston engine, used at a rating of 3,000hp to power the B-36, this improved by the addition of a large turbine driven by the exhaust gases to give over 4,000hp with better fuel economy. The other was a turbo-prop. Pratt & Whitney was trying to build powerful turbo-props, but their rival Wright Aeronautical, was ahead with its T35 Typhoon, a big turboprop rated at 5,500hp that was flight tested fitted in the nose of a B-17 Flying Fortress in September 1947.

In those days there was no known way of designing a jet bomber with significant range to fly the long global missions of the USAF Strategic Air Command. Boeing and other companies were working on jet bombers, but these were relatively short-range aircraft.

The B-47 Stratojet became interesting mainly because its drag was so much less than expected, and because Boeing developed a way of refuelling in-flight. Even then, the B-47 could not fly the longest SAC missions, which of course were directed against the Soviet Union from bases in North America. Throughout 1947-48 Boeing, like the newly created USAF, continued to study long-range jet bombers but never changed their previous conclusion that the only way meet the needs of SAC was to use propellers. Then in 1949, Pratt & Whitney began running a remarkable new turbojet. Later to develop into the J57, it had two sets of turbines and compressors, and instead of compressing its airflow about fives times it compressed it 12.5 times. As in most forms of heat engine, the greater the compression the better the fuel economy. The J57 promised to be dramatically more economical than other turbojets of the era, and it seemed to be a possible key to a long-range jet bomber.

In October 1948, before an engine similar to the J57 had run, Boeing had made a proposal for such an aircraft. It had previously completed a detailed study for a medium bomber with four new jet engines each rated at 3,855kg (8,500lb) of thrust. The basis of the 1948 proposal was in effect a doubling of the medium bomber concept ; instead of four single engine pods it was to have four twin pods. At the time the Boeing Model 464 was possible, but only on paper. The real aircraft would only become a reality when the Pratt & Whitney J57 engines became available, and the fact that eight of them were needed to get the bomber into the air served to underline the problems Boeing faced. With late-1940s technology still prominent in other areas of the design, even with the more effective engines, to build a global strategic bomber was a major challenge.

The first two Boeing Model 464s with USAF designations XB-52 and YB-52 made their appearance in 1952. In fact it was the YB-52 (serial 49-231) that flew first, on 15 April 1952, in the hands of 'Tex' Johnston and Colonel Guy M Townsend (the XB-52 flew six months later), the crew seated in the tandem cockpit similar to its predecessor, later replaced by the more conventional bomber side-by-side arrangement. Three days later the rival, Convair company flew the even bigger YB-60, with eight of the same P&W J57 engines ; but, despite the apparent cost-saving exercise of using almost the same fuselage, landing gear and systems as the piston-engined Convair B-36, the YB-60 (initially designated B-36G) was not adopted by SAC. Instead, the order for the world's first intercontinental jet bomber went to the Boeing Company, because the B-52 already showed the potential to be a superior airplane. It was also a unique airplane in many ways. The sheer size of the airframe caused problems due to sagging and other airframe distortion both in flight and on the ground, and the fin was so tall it had to be made to hinge over sideways so that the B-52 could enter hangars. Instead of a conventional landing gear the weight was taken on four twin-wheel trucks, folding into large compartments in the front and rear sections of the fuselage, and for cross-wind landings all four trucks could be rotated to the correct angle for landing and aligned with the runway even though the massive bomber might be crabbing diagonally down the runway. To support the mighty swept-wings there were outrigger wheels just inboard of the wing-tips. With the enormous fuel load of 29,645 gallons (more in later models) these outriggers press hard into the ground, but at the end of a long mission, with most of the fuel burned and bombs gone, they hung from the wing several feet above the ground. Secondary power was obtained from power packs, distributed throughout the airplane, driven by hot compressed air from the engines, and piped through stainless-steel ducts.

Designed primarily as a high-altitude bomber using gravity-fall nuclear bombs. It progressed to become a platform for Hound Dog stand-off missiles, fought in South-East Asia in the conventional bomber role, became a low-altitude nuclear bomber after the SAM (surface-to-air missile) threat ended high-altitude operations for ever, became a carrier of the Air-Launched Cruise Missile (ALCM) and the carrier of the massive 'bunker buster' bomb for use in the war against terror.

Development of the Stratofortress moved logically through B-52B, C, D, E, F, G and H models, each improved over the others and all powered by the J57 turbojet engines with water injection, which produced the darkest, smokiest take-offs ever seen emitting from a combat aircraft. Watching a pair of B-52s roar into the air on a scramble alert, the bystander could quite easily be blinded and begin to choke from the clouds of carbon bellowing out from the rear of the aircraft. Only the B-52H had TF33-P-3 turbofan engines, which marked a considerable leap forward in technology, sharply reducing the smoke, and providing 30 per cent more power.

In August 1954, the first B-52A appeared, the first of a long line of Stratofortresses to show the changed appearance of the production aircraft. Instead of the two pilots seated in tandem under a curious 12-windowed canopy, they were now side-by-side on a conventional type large airplane flight-deck, both with an upward ejecting seat and the fuselage was lengthened by four feet. Below the pilot and co-pilot were the bombardier and radar operator, while in the extreme tail was a rear gunner in a jettisonable compartment with a radar-controlled battery of four 12.7-mm (0.5-in calibre) guns.

The engines were eight J57-9Ws with water-injection, resulting in maximum take-off thrust of 5,690 kg (12,500lb). The noise and smoke of a B-52 take-off was awe-inspiring, if not a health hazard to the bystander, and a recurrent problem was that the intense noise sometimes caused cracks to appear in the flaps which were depressed between the engines. Gross weight of the A model was 188,244 kg (415,500lb) complete with fixed fuel pods under the outer wings. This was much more than double the aircrafts empty weight. The 13 service-test airplanes ordered were actually delivered as three A models and ten B types for SAC operations, fitted with large and complex MA-2 radar bombing and navigation systems, and with better engines and greater weight. After delivering 23 B-52B and 27 similar aircraft originally ordered as RB-52B bomber-reconnaissance aircraft — planned to have a capability of carrying a two-man pod in the bomb-bay filled with reconnaissance systems — Boeing next built 35 B-52C models with enormous 11,370 litre (2,500 gallon) under-wing tanks. They then went on to build 101 B-52Ds at Seattle and 69 at the Wichita factory, the D having a completely different MD-9 rear defence system. Next came 42 B-52E aircraft from Seattle and 58 from Wichita, with totally new ASQ-38 bomb/navigation system and re-arranged crew. Seattle's last B-52s were 44 F-models, of which a further 45 were produced at Wichita ; among many other changes this had 6,237 kg (13,750lb) J57-43W engines, with titanium compressors, driving the accessories directly instead of via piped bleed air. To permit the accessories to be fitted within the engine pods prominent blisters were introduced.

Originally it had been planned to build 603 B-52s, but extra batches were added of improved models. With the B-52G, first flown in October 1958, Boeing created what was virtually a different airplane. It had a totally different structure, which incorporated integral-tank wings giving roughly twice the capacity of the first XB-52, as well as a much shorter fin. All tail controls were fully powered, and ailerons were eliminated. The gunner was moved into the main crew compartment, with another totally different fire-control system, the AGS-15. The B-52G could carry McDonnell ADM-20 Quail decoy missile in the weapon bay, and under the inner wings were pylons for two of the new AGM-28 Hound Dog missiles (whose J52 engines could be used to assist the bomber to take off). Wichita delivered 193 of these greatly advanced bombers, followed by a further 102 H models. The B-52H had by far the best performance with regards to range, as it was powered by the development of the J57 engine, the TF33 turbofan. Rated at 7,711 kg (17,000lb) thrust, or double the power of the original J57, the TF33 not only enabled the troublesome water-injection system to be eliminated but extended the bombers range by about 30 per cent, due to the engine higher propulsive efficiency. It was also more environmentally friendly, having eliminated all the smoke and noise of take-off, although inside the big bomber it was always a extremely quiet and pleasant aircraft to fly in. The B-52H had been planned to carry four Douglas GAM-87A Skybolt missiles, but this weapon was terminated in December 1962. So for a while the only missile carried on the B-52H was Hound Dog, though it did have the defensive advantage of new ECM (electronic counter-measures) and a 'Gatling' 20-mm quick-fire tail gun.

Since its inception, the B-52 has been called on to meet some very exacting operational requirements world-wide, having remained in front-line service for long after its original planned service lifetime. The toughest period was between 1958-61, when a large portion of the SAC bomber force was kept on constant 'airborne alert' so that it could not be obliterated on the ground by an Soviet ICBM attack on its bases. Next came the dramatic switch from the stratosphere, for which the aircraft was designed, to full-throttle very low level missions. The result was more than a decade of structural problems, and the consequent rebuild and strengthening programmes which cost more than the airplanes originally cost to buy. Then, it was Vietnam, and the aircraft involved — the B-52D and F models — were painted black underneath instead of the nuclear anti-flash white and rebuilt to carry heavier loads of conventional 'iron' bombs. The B-52F kept its weapon bay unchanged, with capacity for twenty-seven bombs of 454kg (1,000lb), and added long racks on Hound Dog type pylons each able to carry four triple 340kg (750lb) bombs. The D model was fitted with external racks to carry twenty-four 500lb bombs but also gained a rebuilt internal 'Big Belly' bay able to carry eighty-four 227kg (500lb) bombs, so that the total bomb-load rose to about 31,750kg (70,000lb). Thousands of long missions were flown to and over the battle areas from bases in Guam in the Marianas and Thailand.

While the General Dynamics FB-111A Aardvark fighter-bomber replaced the B-52A, B, C and E models, many of the D, F, G and H models soldiered on in the SAC bomb wings for another twenty years. They underwent many rebuild and modification cycles, which gave most G and H models the capability to carry the AGM-69A SRAM (Short Range Attack Missile) nuclear weapon for defence suppression during the mission, and later, after a considerable delay AGM-86A Air Launched Cruise Missiles (ALCM). These weapons carried on an internal rotary dispenser.

Under the nose of those H models that remain in the USAF's 21st century inventory, can be seen, the twin bulges of the ASQ-151 electro-optical viewing system, one covering the low-light TV and the other a FLIR (Forward Looking Infra-Red). Ironically, as the coalitions war against terror in Afghanistan and Iraq gathered pace, post-9/11, the B-52 has also reverted to its original role of delivering massive amounts of conventional 'iron' bombs. How history repeats itself !

The incredible evolution of the B-52 and its strategic mission for over half a century can be understood in part by reviewing the many changes in weaponry carried by this remarkable airplane.
In its early missions, to drop gravity bombs on Soviet targets, the B-52 in its spacious bomb-bay could accommodate the monstrous Mk 17, an enormous flat-finned hydrogen bomb capable of 25 megatons of destruction and typical of both the President Eisenhower/Khrushchev era when both West and East seemed intent on building ever more powerful nuclear weapons. One American Mk 17 weapon was tested, when air-dropped by a B-52 at Bikini Atoll during Operation *Redwing,* on 1 May 1956.

The B-52 also carried Mk 28, Mk 36 and Mk 39 nuclear bombs all gigantic weapons, as well as the sleek interim Mk 43. Subsequently, with the onset of *detente* these weapons were replaced by the slim, lower-yield B-28 and B-61 gravity-fall nuclear bombs.

Almost forgotten today, the GAM-87A Skybolt stand-off nuclear missile of 1959-60, a nuclear stand-off weapon intended for use by SAC B-52s and the British RAF Avro Vulcan bomber, was test-flown aboard a SAC B-52H (which would have operated with four Skybolts mounted on the inboard under-wing pylons). Budget problems, trials failures and the inevitable political controversy led to the cancellation of Skybolt and it was never used operationally by SAC or the RAF — but was the predecessor of the air-launched cruise missile.

The GAM-77 (later AGM-28) Hound Dog stand-off missile, in fact, not only became operational but was the principle weapon in SAC's B-52G/H force during 1961-1976. The Hound Dog was a cruise missile (before the term was in use) with an inertial guidance system which could be updated by the B-52's onboard weapons system just before launch. It had a capability to use electronics to confuse Soviet defences, but its primary purpose was to deliver a one-megaton warhead to a target a distance of 500 miles from launch, enabling the bomber to turn away and make good its escape.

An interesting feature of the Hound Dog was that its 6,800lb thrust Pratt & Whitney J52-P-3 engine could be used to give the Stratofortress extra thrust for take-off, since the missile's fuel supply could be replenished in flight from the bomber. By the early 1960s, 593 Hound Dog missiles were in the SAC inventory.

The GAM-72 (later ADM-72) Quail decoy missile was employed by SAC during 1961-78. The Quail was capable of creating a B-52-like radar image on the enemy's screens; it was a stubby missile with folding wings designed to fit in the B-52 bomb-bay, where up to four Quails could be carried in addition to the normal bomb-load. When launched from a B-52 over enemy territory the Quail could fly at about 400 mph over a distance of 400 miles, powered by a 7,000lb thrust General Electric J85-GE-7 turbojet.

In the 1960s as a carrier for the Lockheed GTD-21 'Spy Drone', developed for reconnaissance work embodying many features of the Lockheed A-12 reconnaissance aircraft, forerunner to the supersonic SR-71 Blackbird, B-52H Superfortresses acted as the carrier. Used on intelligence missions in the Far East, these black, demon like drones have never officially been acknowledged to have been deployed operationally, even after a few appeared at a USAF military storage location, and little information is available as to their role, although it is believed to be CIA linked, as were the original A-12 airplanes.
The stand-off missile programme progressed further with the AGM-69 SRAM, in service with SAC since 1972. Twenty SRAM's can be carried on B-52G/H models, as well as on the Rockwell B-1B Lancer. The relatively small, teardrop-shaped SRAM operates very much like a rocket-boosted artillery shell and can be 'lobbed' at targets up to 1,000 miles away.

Finally, the B-52 Stratofortress became the airborne carrier for the AGM-86A Air-Launched Cruise Missile. The weapon also employed by the B-1B Lancer and the B-2A Spirit.

Since the 1950s the B-52 had been the symbol and main instrument of US air power projection around the world. Although the nuclear role always remained to the fore throughout the years, the heavy conventional raids on Vietnam introduced another, more terrifying facet of the big bomber.

'Arc Light' combat operations in South Vietnam began on 18 June 1965 when B-52F Stratofortresses of the 7th and 320th Bomb Wings made the first strike on suspected Viet Cong positions in a disastrous mission in which two bombers collided and crashed.

Over the succeeding years B-52 bombers continued to bomb communist guerrillas in the jungle (or sometimes just the jungle) while USAF fighter-bombers carried the war further north to Hanoi and Haiphong. .

From 1965 until 1972, a somewhat confused war in south-east Asia went on, and while B-52 crews performed admirably — the Stratofortress airmen, originally trained for a strategic role, were eager to be given "real" targets to assault. The use of a nuclear bomber in the conventional role had been totally unforeseen. B-52Fs, which went into the conventional role without preparation, soon turned out to be less than ideal. Under Project 'Big Belly', a number of B-52D bombers were modified to carry up to 108 500lb iron bombs, including 84 located internally in 'clip in' sleeves. By 1967, when General Joseph Nazarro commanded SAC, the Big Belly airplanes were replacing the initial B-52Fs and the daily strikes continued at an increasing rate. Still, B-52 crews were not allowed to 'go north' (to Hanoi) or to hit strategic targets.

When negotiations with North Vietnam broke down, it was decided to remove all restrictions and mount a massive assault against the North to force Hanoi to the negotiating table. The result was the bombing campaign known as The Eleven Days of Christmas or Operation *Linebacker II*.. Over 18-29 December 1972 (with a pause only for Christmas Day), B-52s from Guam and U-Tapao AB, Thailand, struck North Vietnam relentlessly. B-52Ds, which had made up the conventional force, were joined by B-52Gs, which were newer but had not been converted to the conventional role. B-52G pilots did not feel good about having to take the same risk of life to deliver just twenty-seven iron bombs that B-52D pilots took to deliver 108.

Operation *Linebacker II* was also called 'The Eleven Day War', and it was a unique event in history. SAC leaders would not admit it — least of all WW II fighter 'ace' General John C Meyer, who took command of SAC on 1 May 1972), but in order to commit nearly 50 per cent of the B-52 force against Hanoi, SAC squadrons were 'stripped' of their nuclear capability. At Andersen AFB, Guam, at least three times the number of bombers which had been considered the base's maximum went into action. Operating in cells of three, B-52s struck targets in North Vietnam in the face of intense resistance from MiG-21 air defence fighters and SAMs. After eight years of war without casualties, no fewer than eighteen B-52s were shot down by SAMs, while two MiG-21s fell to the bombers' guns.

Nevertheless, the massive B-52 operation inflicted heavy damage to North Vietnam and resulted in the war being ended by a political settlement on 27 January 1973. Now, the B-52 returned to strategic business, — although a variety of conventional roles were developed in the 1980s. SAC planners turned their attention, once again, to the chief problem — how to penetrate Soviet air defences.

Development of an offensive avionics system (OAS) first flown in a B-52G on 3 September 1980, amounted in effect to a rebuild of the entire interior of the B-52 to make it capable of operating in its new role of low-level strategic attack. By 1980, another bomber intended to replace the B-52 — the Rockwell B-1A — had been cancelled, and it appeared the B-52 would have to soldier on in the global bombing role forever.

Subsequently, the Stratofortress, was modified and upgraded to cover every contingency to attack strategic targets, with nuclear or conventional weapons. These included free-fall unguided bombs and a range of air-to-surface missiles, including the Israeli AGM-142 Popeye (US 'Have Nap'), AGM-84 Harpoon anti-ship missiles and the AGM-86C, a conventional GPS-guided version of the Boeing Air-Launched Cruise Missile. These weapons were mainly carried by B-52G — the last of which was withdrawn from store in 1994 — but could also be carried by the newer B-52H variant. The B-52H at this time normally carried either the nuclear-armed AGM-86B cruise missile, which navigates using terrain contour-matching, or the newer AGM-129 advanced cruise missile. Such weapons, and the lightweight, slender free-fall B-28 and free-fall B-61 nuclear bombs, were decidedly 'lightweight' to the huge 25-megaton Mk 17s around which the original B-52 Stratofortress was designed.

Originally the Stratofortress was conceived as a nuclear weapon carrier and not a conventional bomber -- but the latter capability was soon developed in particular to deploy the bomber to south-east Asia to take part in the *Arc Light/Linebacker* bombing offensive in Vietnam. Most of these missions were flown against targets in the South and North Vietnam panhandle adjacent to the de-militarised zone (DMZ). In addition, repeated deep penetrations were made into North Vietnam particularly to the well fortified port of Haiphong and the heavily defended industrial complex around Hanoi. During nearly all these missions the bomber was subjected to heavy SAM threats around these centres, anti-aircraft batteries, and the latest Soviet Mikoyan interceptors.

Starting in 1961, SAC implemented its 24-hour nuclear airborne and ground alert policy. It was a bold move that was enough to convince the Soviet Union of America's resolve to defend itself against the threat posed by the world-wide aspirations of the communist regime in power at the time. Such airborne missions became commonplace for SAC B-52 crews and normally involved two airborne refuellings. Crews remained aloft for 24 tiring hours at a time, usually orbiting high in the North Polar region, awaiting an authenticated 'go' code message to proceed to their pre-assigned targets in the Soviet Union. All co-ordinated through an elaborate airborne and ground 'positive control command system', under the direct control of the President of the United States, through the Joint Chiefs of Staff to SAC H.Q., and ultimately the bomber crews.

At the same time back at home, colleagues remained on a constant state of readiness seven days a week around the clock — their airplanes bombed-up, targets selected and allocated, the aircraft poised for a massive counter blow, ready to launch at 15-second intervals, as a retaliatory back-up strike force. The Soviets knew the United States was ready to hit back, should they launch a pre-emptive strike on continental USA. Fortunately that never happened.

In the main, due to the highly successful SAC B-52 airborne and ground alert operations during the periods of high tension. The bombers were augmented by the full complement of the countries other deterrent, the ICBM unit's that maintained a constant watch on the Soviet Union.

SAC's primary mission throughout it long and distinguished history — was to deter war, or should it occur, to destroy the enemy's will and ability to fight. To implement the old adage, 'Preparedness is the answer to potential aggressors'.

SAC was the USAF's largest Command, with 121,000 personnel and a 260 B-52 bomber force spread within the Commands two numbered air forces — the 8th Air Force at Barksdale under Lt Gen Ellie G Shuler Jr, and the 15th Air Force at March AFB, California, under Lt Gen Richard A Burpee.

A SAC press release of 11 May 1988 announced newly-assigned conventional bombing roles for the 62nd Bomb Squadron of the 2nd Wing (Barksdale), as well as the 43rd Bomb Wing (Andersen), and the 320th Wing (Mather).

B-52G models intended for the conventional mission could also carry AGM-84A Harpoon air-to-surface missiles, a new addition to the Stratofortress armoury at this time. One squadron of fifteen B-52s based on Guam so equipped, conducted maritime anti-shipping missions in the Pacific. Another in Maine in the United States did the same job in the Atlantic. Other units carried a 'clip' of four B-61 free-fall nuclear weapons in the B-52s aft bomb-bay, an arrangement which left the forward bay available for counter-measures devices, extra fuel, or other equipment needed for a long-range mission. The sleek B-61 weapon is a 'maximum drogued' bomb to be retarded during a low-level drop to give the bombers crew time to escape the drop zone.

It was stated by the Pentagon at this time, that consideration had been given to using B-52s on the 15 April 1986 air strikes against terrorist-related targets in Libya, the aircraft taking off from the United States sparing any need to use foreign airfields or impinge on another nations airspace. F-111 fighter-bombers launched from RAF Lakenheath and Upper Heyford in the UK, to strike targets in Libya, were refused over-flight permission during Operation *El Dorado Canyon* by France. It is believed the B-52s would have been a better bet to strike at Libya's Rabta chemical plant.

Most B-52 strike missions are flown at night as were the 'Shock and awe' missions against Baghdad during Gulf War II, to increase the element of surprise, the big bomber's tremendous range permitting it to come from a direction totally unexpected and to avoid any SAMs, radar-guided missiles or anti-aircraft guns.

It is ironical that in a war in which the extraordinary capabilities of 'smart' weapons were demonstrated in full for the first time, that the B-52, veteran of the Vietnam War more than thirty years earlier, played an important part once again.

From the start of Operation *Desert Shield* in August 1990 around 30 B-52Gs from the 69th BS, 42nd Bombardment Wing at Loring AFB, Maine, and the 328th BS, 93rd BW from Castle AFB, California were deployed to the island of Diego Garcia in the Indian Ocean. These bombers started combat operations on the night of 17 January 1991, dropping thirteen tons of high explosive on armament factories in central Iraq.

From then on, both by day and night, formations of from two to five B-52Gs continued to attack strategic targets in northern Iraq. From the second week of the operations they extended their targets from strategic sites to include the Iraqi Army, particularly Republican Guard units in northwest Kuwait. The third week brought a slight change in targeting with the bombers attacking Iraqi mechanised units moving up to the Saudi border. With Saddam Hussein's intentions at this time apparently to lure the coalition into a premature ground war.

Despite its age, the B-52G at this time was quite a modern weapon system, it having been progressively upgraded right up to 1989. The Offensive Avionics System (OAS) update in 1987 embodied a significant increase in the bombers capability. Sixty-nine of the B-52Gs in the SAC inventory received a terrain-following radar almost identical to that used in the Tomahawk cruise missile. A defensive aids ECM system that could handle sixteen enemy radars, and jam at least twelve of them simultaneously. Two pods were fitted under the nose: one contained a low-light TV camera and the other an FLIR — the ALQ-172 Pave Mint, developed by ITT avionics. In the rear of the bomber a radar system was installed that was capable of detecting when the aircraft had been illuminated by an enemy radar — either from an interceptor or a missile — and launching chaff or flares for self-defence.

In addition to the avionic upgrades the bombers offensive armament was modernised with the aircraft capable of carrying a range of ordnance including: Mk 82 500lb 'iron bomb' (27 in the bomb-bay and 24 on under-wing hard-points) to the new AGM-142A 'Have Nap' air-to-surface missile and the AGM-88 HARM anti-radar missile. The Harm permitting the bomber to fire ahead, 'to blind' its target so that it can bomb without danger from the enemy's ground-based defences. Several B-52Gs of the 93rd Bomb Wing, 328th BS, from Castle AFB, California used HARM missiles during the first few days of 'Desert Storm'.

On 2 February a B-52G of 4300th BW(P) from the 42nd BW Loring AFB, was lost over the Indian Ocean. Believed to be to due mechanical causes when the aircraft was returning from its mission, giving rise to a massive electrical failure during the landing approach to Diego Garcia. Three crew were rescued, one was confirmed dead, two missing.

During Gulf War 1 Boeing B-52s flew 1,624 missions, dropping 25,700 tons of bombs — 29 percent of the total tonnage delivered during the war. Flying from their forward operating bases, they attacked targets such as troop concentrations, airfields, factories, munitions storage areas, rail yards and minefields. On average each bomber launched with nine M-117 low drag General Purpose bombs on each of its Heavy Stores Adapter Beams (HSABs) and another twenty-seven in the bomb-bay.

The B-52 carried out the longest bombing raids in history on the first day of the war, when seven aircraft launched thirty-five cruise missiles against targets in Iraq. The AGM-86C ALCM, carrying conventional warheads, were targeted against air defence sites around Mosul (Saddam Hassein's home town) in northern Iraq in a mission involving B-52s of the 2nd Bomb Wing operating 35 hour 20 minute 'round robin' flights direct from their base at Barksdale AFB, Louisiana. However, most 'Buffs' taking part in *Desert Storm* carried conventional 'iron' bombs from bases in the UK, Spain, Diego Garcia and Saudi Arabia.

During Gulf War II over ten years later eight B-52Hs from the 5th BW, 23rd BS based at Minot AFB, North Dakota, arrived at RAF Fairford in the UK on 3 March 2003. The following day a further six 5th BW B-52H arrived at Fairford bringing the total complement of UK-based 'Buffs' to 14. In addition, the 2nd BW B-52Hs that included the 11th BS, 20th BS, and 96th BS deployed to Diego Garcia and around twelve aircraft from Barksdale AFB were deployed to Guam as a show of force against North Korea. Rockwell B-1B Lancers from the 28th BW, Ellsworth AFB, South Dakota, deployed to Oman and Diego Garcia. Up to 16 Northrop B-2A Spirits from 509th BW, Whiteman AFB, Missouri, deployed to Diego Garcia. The bombers incorporated into Expeditionary Wings

In 2004, the USAF retained 76 Boeing B-52H bombers in operational service the airplanes planned to remain in use until 2045. By that time the youngest airframe will be 80 years old. 102 H-models having been built between 1960-1961. Around 50 B-52H are in front-line USAF service at any one time. The airframe has an estimated fatigue life of 37,500 hours, limited primarily by the wing upper skin. Boeing is studying the possibility of a complete rewiring and glass cockpit upgrade. In the interim, the AMI (Avionics Midlife Improvement) replaces the inertial navigation system (INS) with a enhanced Honeywell strap-down system. For low-level terrain-following sorties, the pilots wear NVGs (Night Vision Goggles).

Other AMI work includes replacing processors to increase memory and data throughput, as well as upgrading flight and weapons system software. At the same time the Situational Awareness Defensive Improvement (SADI) upgrade of the bomber's low/medium-band ECM equipment is underway. This will replace the ALR-20 receiver with the Lockheed Martin ALQ-210 equipment. Replacement of the ALR-46 rear-warning-receiver (RWR) is also being considered.

Funding is being sought to add Link 16 and EHF communications from 2004. Adding datalink is a pre-requisite for the planned Enhanced Bomber Mission Management programme, which would allow weapons to be re-assigned and re-targeted whilst the bomber was airborne en-route the target area.
Adding weapons to the B-52s repertoire is relatively inexpensive because of its size and load carrying capacity. Wind Corrected Munitions Dispenser (WCMD) and Joint Direct Attack Munition(JDAM) are carried externally. Although it is intended to extend the 'J-series' 1760 databus-type conventional weapons capability in the bomb-bay. Joint Stand-Off Weapon (JSOW) and Joint Air-to-Surface Stand-Off Missile (JASSM) was added in 2003. Boeing's Phantom Works is using the type to test the new experimental 15 ton Massive Ordnance Penetrator weapon

The USAF is still re-considering whether it will re-engine the airplanes; the four engine pylons each with two Pratt & Whitney TF33-P-3 turbofans. Proposals include fitment of US-assembled Rolls-Royce RB-211-535s; P&W PW2000s, which would be common with the Boeing/MDC C-17 Globemaster III F-117 powerplants; or General Electric CF6s common to the Lockheed C-5 Galaxy strategic transport.
The air force is also considering creating an EB-52 variant fitted with a low-band jammer to protect the F-117 Nighthawks against the latest EW threats, as well as embodying the type with the capability to operate in conjunction with the Grumman EA-6B, Boeing EA-18G and UAVs to jam enemy communications and radars. A tentative in-service date for sixteen airplanes has been muted as 2012.

Chapter 4   B-52 Training School

For Strategic Air Command, the 93rd Bomb Wing at Castle AFB, became the major Boeing B-52 training facility, for upgrading crew members selected to fly the 'Buff' — Big Ugly Fat Fellow —, from the vast network of SAC heavy bomber bases across the United States. Most crew members in the early 1950s came from units flying Boeing B-47 Stratojets, or the piston-engined Convair B-36s, Boeing B-50s and B-29s.

On arrival at Castle, after six weeks of ground school training in B-52 operational systems, B-52 simulator, and familiarisation in the B-52 procedures with the 4017th Combat Crew Training Squadron, the crews were made ready to make their first flight in the Stratofortress.

The 93rd Bomb Wing was the first USAF unit to fully convert to B-52s. This was the principal reason it was chosen as SAC's primary B-52 training unit. In addition to its training mission, however, the 93rd (a famous WW II USAAF Bomber Wing) was also a full combat unit. Crews of the 4017th Training Squadron and the 328th, 329th and 330th Bomb Squadrons at Castle, were formed into instructor teams for training new incoming crew members. In addition to their regular training assignments, each of the 93rd Bomb Wing squadrons had combat missions consistent with the Strategic Air Command War Plan.

Many newly assigned training crews had flown together for many years in B-29s, B-50s, B-36s etc, and would eventually return to their home bases. A number, who were designated to remain at Castle to become B-52 instructors, were selected on their flying background, previous instructor experience, and a number of other different factors. All, were required to complete ten instructor-supervised training missions in 35 days. If the crew successfully completed a rigorous standardisation check ride on mission ten, the crew would be allowed to fly together as a qualified solo crew on two missions, but only after passing a satisfactory interview with the squadron commander. Pre-designated instructor crews, as well as crews returning to their own units and other assignments, flew approximately the same initial ten supervised training missions. Instructor designated crews were given supplemental duties in various aspects of instructional techniques peculiar to the 'Buff'.

Initially SAC's 93rd Bomb Wing at Castle received 50 B models produced by Boeing at Seattle and this model became the mainstay at the base until the C Model began to leave the production line in March 1956. The two models were similar except that the latter could carry an additional 41,700 gallons (157,850 litres) of fuel increasing its gross weight to 450,000lb (204,000kg).

Later, in May 1956 the first D models arrived at Castle, most of which were produced at Boeing's Wichita plant in Kansas. This particular model received the so-called 'Big Belly' modification which increased its conventional bomb-carrying capability to eighty-four 227kg (500lb) bombs carried internally and twenty-four 340kg (750lb) bombs under the wings.

C and D variants were the primary types operated in south-east Asia during the Vietnam War, by units operating out of Guam, Thailand and Okinawa. Subsequently, in Castle's history, additional models of the 'Buff' were operated from the base for crew training and combat mission assignments, from the 'A' model through to the turbofan-powered 'H' model.

The second unit to be assigned B-52s was the 42nd Bomb Wing at Loring AFB, in Maine, converting from piston-engined Convair B-36s. Over a number of years SAC phased in 36 Bomb Wings equipped with the Boeing B-52 Stratofortress. The particular model flown dependant on the combat mission allocated the unit.

In total, 757 B-52s were built, from the roll-out of the first 'A' model until the last 'H' model which came off the production line in September 1960. It is of interest to compare the 'H' model Stratofortresses massive 17,000lbs of thrust performance with the USAF's first jet bomber the North American B-45 Tornado, with its four Allison-built J35-A-11 of a mere 4.000lb thrust.

Still flying after nearly five decades of operational service the B-52 still remains at the forefront of America's was against terror. The 'Buff' travels at 1,050 km/h (650 mph), at altitudes around 15,240 metres (50,000ft) and is capable of carrying both conventional and nuclear weapons as well as cruise missiles, and massive bunker busting bombs.

Early models had an un-refuelled range of 9,650 km (6,000 miles). Later models increased that range to more than 19,300 km (12,000 miles). With the addition of in-flight refuelling, the B-52's range is limited only by crew fatigue. In the B-52G and H models, the latter of which is still flying today in 2006, the gunner's position has been moved from the tail to the forward section of the bomber, with a television camera mounted in the tail section and used for fire control.

Chapter 5 Pacific Nuclear Tests - Operation *Redwing* and *Hardtack*

Pacific nuclear tests Operation *Redwing* and *Hardtrack* was the detonation of sixteen nuclear warheads at Eniwetok and Bikini Atolls from May to July 1956. These explosions included two air-dropped hydrogen bombs by Boeing B-52 Stratofortress and Convair B-36 Peacemaker aircraft — the early catastrophic 'Cherokee' shot of May 1956 by the B-52, and the 'Osage' shot of 16 June 1956, dropped by a B-36. *Redwing* also tested the nuclear weapon explosions effects on US warplanes then in front-line service, including, for the first time the B-52.

It was however, not the first time the Americans had gone to the Pacific to unleash the might of an atomic weapon. But, it was the first test series involving the B-52 and the first aerial drop by the USAF of a thermonuclear bomb — although the Soviets had airdropped such a weapon six months earlier. Two Pacific test series that came later, Operations *Hardtack* and *Dominie*, also involved B-52s.

The first B-52B (serial 56-0004), nicknamed 'The Tender Trap' was instrumented to evaluate the effects of nuclear blasts on the bomber. Testing the effects of weapon detonations on aircraft had begun with Operation *Cross-roads* in the Marshall Islands in 1946, with drone Boeing B-17s. The XB-47 Stratojet, two B-50s and a B-47B performed the first tests of aircraft structures against the very big multi-megaton weapons in Operations *Ivy* and *Castle* in 1952 and 1955. (The Ivy Mike blast of 1 November 1952, that wiped out the island of Elugelab, was the world's first thermonuclear detonation but was a cab-mounted device, not an air-delivered weapon).

To prepare for the Pacific tests, Captain Gene Deatrick, a Wright Field, Air Development Centre (WADC) test pilot, went to Seattle to check out in the B-52. In his first flight on a B-52 in June 1955, Deatrick found the bomber heavy on the controls but comfortable, stable, and forgiving. To Deatrick the B-47, was the ideal bomber, 'the last 'fighter' a bomber pilot could fly'. The B-52 being more of a stretched limousine'. When test pilot Lt-Col Guy M Townsend (who made the first flight of the YB-52 on 15 April 1952 with Tex Johnston) signed off Deatrick on the B-52 type in August 1955. Deatrick felt he was now qualified in the 'Cadillac of the Skies.

Although, in Deatrick's view, the bomber wasn't perfect. A major design error had placed the airplanes four bleed-air driven alternators in its bomb-bay. This arrangement used pneumatic power for operation of major accessories, bleeding air from the engines and piping it through the aircraft to energise the hydraulics, electrics, air conditioning, engine water injection, and de-icing. The more troublesome of the two alternator models in use had turbine blades which froze — blamed for the early loss of a bomber which Colonel Pat Fleming vice-commander of the 93rd Bomb Wing at Castle AFB, California was flying. Aware of the problem, the Pentagon vowed it would 'not spend another dime for this B-52 aircraft until a fix was found', But, it was not until the 389th Stratofortress was delivered a B-52G model, that the alternators were moved up to the engine nacelles.

In March 1956, with Wright Field test pilot Major Charles G 'Andy' Anderson as pilot and Deatrick as co-pilot and with a new designation JB-52B, 'The Tender Trap' left Seattle for Eniwetok. It is believed this was the first B-52 to leave the United States.

Wright Field despatched the JB-52, a B-47E, a B-57, a B-66, an F-101 and two F-84s. From Albuquerque a dozen Martin B-57 Canberras were despatched to gather nuclear samples. At tiny Eniwetok, there were Douglas C-47s, and C-54 transports, and H-19 and SA-16 helicopters.

The crew of 'The Tender Trap' (JB-52, serial 52-0004) were tasked to monitor three effects during the weapons-effect test flying at Eniwetok Atoll in 1956 — radiation, heat, and the shock wave. The crew of a B-52B (serial 52-0013) from Albuquerque had the job of releasing the air-dropped weapon known as Cherokee on 16 May 1956, when two bombs were detonated on a single day.

With the bomb-drop B-52B and the JB-52 located at the crowded Eniwetok airstrip, the ground crews were relieved to find the Stratofortress easier to handle than expected. With its massive, wide, drooping wings they were surprised the bombers were easy to turn and manoeuvre on the ramp.
The bomb dropped on 16 May 1956, was a Mk 15 Zombie thermonuclear bomb released by President Eisenhower, for test, from the war fighting stockpile. Properly released after careful use of the B-52's excellent radar navigation/bombing system, the Cherokee shot, should have reached Ground Zero (an illuminated slab on Namu Island at Bikini Atoll, 200 miles east of Eniwetok) with precise accuracy. It didn't.
Watched by selected members of the press aboard USS *Mount McKinley,* B-52 serial 52-0013 dropped Zombie from 40,000 feet and detonated it at 4,350 feet, producing a 3.75 megaton blast. Records revealed, at detonation the bomb missed its target by 5,882 metres (129,000ft) because it was dropped 21 seconds too early when the bombardier mistook another lighted island for the Ground Zero site.

The B-52s bombardier made a major mistake. In addition to the target's large cross-shape of lights, there was another small island in the bombers flight path that had a light on it, not a cross but a single point of light. On his original run-in the bombardier sighted on this point, located beyond the proper target. He realised his mistake and moved the cross-hairs of his telescope from the wrong target to the correct one but he made an additional mistake — by not disconnecting the bombing system's computer during the rapid movement of the telescope. The bombing system interpreted this as a sudden increase in ground speed and released the weapon early.

Captain Thomas M Sumner was aircraft commander of the Wright Field B-47E effects-test Stratojet serial 54-2389, nick-named 'Bubba Boy'. Sumner remembers that the 'drop B-52B' crew practised very little and we never had a dress rehearsal.

The call to indicate the drop was completed was 'COMPLETE'. This meant the weapon was out of the B-52B serial 52-0013 bomb-bay and falling. To the horror of the monitoring B-47E and JB-52B crews the call was heard 30 seconds *before* it was scheduled.

This meant the weapon would detonate 30 seconds too early and the monitoring aircraft would be too close. This could lead to the destruction of the aircraft. All the crews could do was to increase speed as much as possible up to the Mach limit of the aircraft. This wasn't enough.

It took the Cherokee weapon 54 seconds to fall. When it exploded the heat was felt inside the bombers and the light was very bright in spite of the blast curtains made of asbestos. The crews were certain their airplanes were on fire and would come apart. They knew ejection was out of the question as this, would mean an even worse fate. In the event, both the B-47 and the JB-52B were beaten about, but both survived.

It was reported that after landing B-52 serial 52-0013 crew left immediately for the United States. But, on arrival in New Mexico they were ordered to return to Eniwetok for an investigation of their bombardier's error...

As *Redwing* continued, JB-52B 'The Tender Trap', was the only Stratofortress in the Pacific at this time. Deatrick's crew continued to expose their aircraft to radiation, intense heat and blast as scientists detonated ground-barge and tower-mounted nuclear and thermonuclear devices. The low-yield Osage shot was dropped by a B-36 over Runit Island at Eniwetok on 16 June 1956.

'The Tender Trap' was airborne when the 70-kiloton Osage test article detonated accurately and produced a 'mushroom' cloud 21,000ft high. Till now it seemed pilots had proved that they could fly and fight in a nuclear environment. But things went wrong when the Dakota shot was detonated in Bikini lagoon south of Yurochi Island on 26 June 1956. This thermonuclear blast produced a radioactive cloud rising to 82,000ft which was 20 miles wide.

To set the JB-52 down on Eniwetok's short runway, a mere 6,500ft in length, it needed full flaps to stop the bomber. If anything untoward happened during flight, the pilots were afraid to lower the flaps, as they knew if they jammed they would be committed, unable to divert to some alternative location in the Pacific.

Flying five miles from the drop zone when the Dakota shot went off, a B-47E Stratojet suffered moderate overpressure damage to its bomb-bay doors and forward landing gear doors and thermal damage to its control surfaces.

'The Tender Trap' bomb-bay doors, flaps, landing gear, brakes and braking parachute were damaged by thermal effects and overpressure. The JB-52 was diverted to Hickham AFB, Hawaii where they landed without brakes or chute.

Now, the evidence was clear, a B-52 bomber could be five miles from a nuclear detonation and still could be damaged by the blast and heat. On the other hand the effects tests by 'The Tender Trap' and 'Bubba Boy', although not without mishap proved that other aircraft could operate within the region of a nuclear detonation. However, at this time all loads and effects on the JB-52 had been with its tail pointing towards the point of detonation. What the experts wanted, was to expose the Stratofortress to a nuclear blast from its front and side.

Operation *Hardtack* was the next series of detonations in the Pacific, carried out at Eniwetok, Bikini and Johnston Island between 28 April and August 1958. Early plans for *Hardtack* included an airdrop by a B-52 Stratofortress of a 25,000 lb thermonuclear weapon to yield 25 megatons and to be the largest detonation ever made by the United States. This was changed and, in the end, *Hardtack* included no airdrops.

As a result, for *Hardtack,* there was only one B-52 in attendance, which was also the only effects-test aircraft. Experts felt they had enough data on all operational US aircraft except the B-52, and a new model of the bomber, the B-52D, was chosen to be exposed to the blasts. The effects-test aircraft, B-52D serial 56-0591 *'Tommy's Tigator'*, captained by Tom Sumner, flew in just nine of the series of 35 ground-based detonations, not including one that was taken to 78,080 metres (252,000ft) by a Redstone missile.

However, having flown a number of successful missions during *Hardtack,* gathering excellent data at various angles, direct side on, at nine o'clock positions relative to the fuselage plus the ten and seven o'clock positions, and some tail load positions to verify data gathered during *Redwing,* having survived a near disaster during the last *Hardtack* shot, later in July 1959, *Tommy's Tigator* crashed in Oregon, killing a Boeing crew.

Chapter 6   Convair B-36 Peacemaker

Although the B-36 Peacemaker's range and speed did not meet USAF specifications it entered service with the 11th Bomb Wing (Heavy) at Carswell AFB, Texas on 18 November 1948 and attained IOC in August 1949. In due course, eleven SAC wings operated the B-36 or the RB-36 reconnaissance variant. In the 1950s, SAC bombers flew routinely with atomic bombs on board while others sat on runway alert. Inevitably this resulted in the occasional mishap, as over Oklahoma in 1958, when a B-36 inadvertently dropped an hydrogen bomb.

Fortunately no accident ever resulted in a nuclear explosion and the global force of 385 B-36s transformed SAC from an empty shell into the most powerful bomber force in the world. There is no doubt that the B-36 certainly deterred Moscow at this time and it lived up to the SAC slogan "Peace is Our Profession".

The B-36 Peacemaker was the first bomber with a truly strategic capability to serve with any air force, the aircraft flew for the first time on 25 August 1946, powered by six Pratt & Whitney R-4630-25 Wasp Major engines in 'pusher' configuration developing 3,000hp each, with large intakes in the wing leading edge to provide cooling air. The engines driving 19ft diameter three-blade Curtiss variable pitch propellers. Maximum speed was 346 mph; cruising speed 216 mph; service ceiling 36,000ft; and range of 9,500 miles with a 10,000lb bomb-load. The two-deck forward cabin housed most of the crew of 15, including two pilots, two flight engineers, navigator, radio operator, radar bombardier and an observer/radar technician.

Truly 'intercontinental' in range the B-36 was the mainstay of SAC in the late 1940s and early 1950s. Dubbed the 'Peacemaker' to this day the aircraft holds the distinction of the world's largest bomber. The aircraft was designed to a 1941 specification for an aircraft capable of bombing Germany from continental USA, carrying a 4,545 kg (10,000lb) bomb-load over a range of 16,000 km (10,000 miles) at speeds between 480 and 640 km/h (300 and 400 mph). To deliver bombs onto Eastern European targets from bases in the United States.

The prototype XB-36 (serial 42-13570) flew in August 1946 piloted by Convair's chief test pilot Beryl Erickson, and was followed by one pre-production YB-36 (serial 42-13571) on 4 December 1947, with a raised cockpit and main landing gear units with four-wheel bogies, and by 21 B-36As with R-4360-25 engines but no armament. These were assigned to the 7th Bomb Group, Carswell AFB between June 1948 and February 1949, to be used a crew trainers. General LeMay placed a 'top secret' classification on the armament and capabilities of these early bombers, to suggest to the Soviet Union that SAC's nuclear delivery capability was greater than it actually was at this time.

There were many problems with the aircraft, including the proverbial engine overheating, propeller malfunctions, fuel and oil leaks, airborne fires, and pressurisation failures. Subsequent rectification work and modifications resulted in a lifecycle cost for the 383 B-36s built of $3,800,000 per aircraft.

The first production B-36A serial 44-92004 made its first flight on 28 August 1947. The operational versions were 73 B-36Bs with 3,500hp R-4360-41 radials. 86 B-36Ds — including 64 conversions — with two turbojets in two under-wing pods for greater speed. Twenty-four RB-36D strategic reconnaissance aircraft — including seven R-36B conversions. 22 RB-36Es — all conversions, 34 B-36Fs with more powerful R-3460-53 radials, 24 RB-36Fs with more fuel, 83 B-36Hs and 73 RB-36Hs with improved flight-decks, and 33 B-36Js with more fuel and strengthened landing gear.

The 22 RB-36E conversions beginning in 1950, were the 21 B-36As and the pre-production YB-36. These airplanes were not built with the thicker skins of the succeeding series models and were subject to the loosening and peeling of skin sections. Air Force sheet metal specialist checked each modified B-36A prior and after each flight, tightening loose skin sections. Fuel leaks were a constant problem, with spilling fuel on the hard-standings commonplace. Ground-crews were continually cleaning up fuel spills, often hosing down the hardstands — something that would not be tolerated today due to safety and environmental health reasons. With upgrade to RB-36E standard the A Models were fitted with six P&W R-43600-41 piston engines and four J47-GE-19 turbojets.

Powerplant modifications allowed the RB-36E and other modified bombers to use water injection on take-off to enable them to use almost any existing airfield. This allowed SAC the choice of operating its bombers from virtually any homeland airfield, thereby complicating the Soviet air forces bomber attack options. Even though re-engined bombers could operate at 42,500ft altitude and attain a top speed of 318 mph, overall performance remained below USAF requirements. It was the size of the aircraft bomb-bays which ensured its continued existence at this time. Each bomb-bay was 30ft in length — able to hold one 42,000 lb 'Grand Slam' hydrogen bomb, and it was the only bomber able to deliver such a weapon.

The B-36B was the USAF's final, piston-engined intercontinental bomber. This was despite the Soviets MiG-15 fighter interceptors operational ceiling approaching 51,000ft and maximum speed of 665 mph which remained somewhat of a threat to the bomber. Finally, the bombers powerplant upgrade with the addition of the two General Electric J47-GE-19 turbojet engines (each rated at 5,200lb s. t.) mounted outboard of the pusher engines, increased performance to a maximum speed of 435 mph at 45,000ft and decreased take-off distance by 2,000ft ! Unfortunately the turbojets and other modifications raised the bombers weight to 385,000 lb, resulting in higher fuel consumption and reduced range.

The B-36D variant used the 'B' model configuration with two more J47 turbojets added, the first ten-engine intercontinental bomber, the airplane referred to by the crew — the 'six turning and four burning'. If fitted with two auxiliary bomb-bay tanks this model had an airborne endurance of approximately forty-eight hours.

The reconnaissance variant became known as the RB-36D. Its two bomb-bays were fitted with eight photo cameras, 80 flash bombs for night photography, electronic counter-measures equipment, auxiliary fuel tanks, and it had a crew of twenty-two. Twenty-four RB-36Ds were assigned to the 28th Strategic Reconnaissance Group at Ellsworth AFB, South Dakota.

Lessons learned in WW II showed it was important that long-range bombers had fighter protection, even one as heavily armed as the 15 machine-gunned B-36. Jet fighter escorts for the B-36 were impractical, the combat range of the new jet fighters coming into service post-WW II were measured in hundreds, rather than the thousands of miles, of the missions envisaged for the B-36. The old idea of a 'parasite fighter' to be carried in the aircrafts bomb-bay was muted, in that the fighter would be released near the combat zone to escort the bomber and then return to the safety of the bomb-bay to return home with the B-36.

In October 1945, a contract was awarded to McDonnell to produce a parasite fighter. The result was one of the strangest aircraft in aviation history. With the restrictions imposed by the need to fit into the B-36s enclosed bomb-bay, the resulting design the XF-85 (of which two prototypes were built) aptly named 'Goblin', The Goblin was in essence an 'egg' with folding wings and held the distinction of being the world's smallest jet fighter a distinction it still holds today, in 2006.

Eventually, however, the parasite fighter chosen to mate with the B-36 was the Republic F-84E Thunderjet and later its swept-wing derivative the, F-84F Thunderstreak. The hooking mechanism for the parasite F-84 was an 'H' shaped trapeze, which was lowered to launch and retrieve the F-84. Once attached, the F-84 was raised into the semi-proud position in the bomb-bay of the B-36 for refuelling or to allow the F-84 pilot to exit the airplane. Testing of the hooking system began in January 1952 and over the next year 170 successful launches and retrievals were made.

In May 1953, Convair and Republic were contracted to convert ten B-36 bombers and 25 RF-84F and F-84K Thunderstreaks to the parasite role, though the fighters role had been subtly changed in the interim. Instead of just being a fighter escort to the B-36, the new role for the RF-84F was for a reconnaissance fighter to the RB-36D strategic reconnaissance aircraft. It was envisioned that the RB-36 would carry the Thunderstreak 4,480 km (2,800 miles) towards the target, then release the RF-84 which was equipped with five cameras to fly over the target at 960 km/h (600 mph). This procedure extending the range of the RB-36 by a further 1,920 km (1,200 miles) in an essentially 'stand-off' reconnaissance role.

By 1955, parasite fighters equipped two Strategic Reconnaissance Wings, the 99th at Fairchild AFB, and the 91st at Larson AFB, both units based in Washington State. However, barely a year into active service the SR Wings were disbanded. As the new Boeing jet bombers entered SAC service, the B-36 was rendered obsolete and with its passing, the need for the parasite fighter disappeared.

It is frequently pointed out that the 70.0 metres (230ft) wing-span of the Comvair B-36 is itself greater than the distance flown by the Wright Brothers during man's first powered flight. Everything about the B-36 was *big* : wing area was 4,772 sq ft. The six Pratt & Whitney R-4360-41 radial piston engines were fed by eight fuel tanks. The bomber had eight gun turrets, four bomb-bays, a fuselage length of 49.40 metres (162ft 1in), a maximum gross weight of no less than 410,000lb.

SAC officers claimed the B-36 had a range of 10,000 miles, enough to reach the Soviet Union carrying the enormous hydrogen bombs developed in the 1950s. In the era before the development of SAMs the B-36 could penetrate Soviet airspace at high-altitude, where fuel consumption was optimum, defend itself with batteries of remotely-operated 20mm cannon, and easily reach and strike any target in the USSR, whether it was Moscow or Andyr (the latter a VVS strategic forces' base in Siberia). Even the new Soviet Mikoyan MiG-15 fighters were unable to climb to altitude to intercept the B-36.

Some B-36s were 'feather-weighted' by removing all armament except the tail guns and reducing the crew from fifteen to nine men. These airplanes could fly so high that in the very thin upper air the higher wing loading of the MiG fighters put the smaller airplanes at a serious disadvantage. To such an extent it was soon decided that altitude was more important than guns. It is believed these airplanes reached an unofficial altitude of 58,000ft. Though, when the Soviet's introduced their new Mikoyan MiG-17 'Fresco' interceptor this altitude safety margin disappeared.

The B-36H/RB-36H was the most prolific variant built, but it had a serious design flaw — at altitudes above 25,000ft, interior pressurised bulkheads had a tendency to fail. Until the bulkheads were reinforced these airplanes were restricted to altitudes below 25,000ft and were not available for long-range penetration missions into the heavily defended Soviet airspace.

The B-36J was the final variant, fitted with one additional fuel tank in each outer wing panel and with strengthened landing gear to support increased weight to 410,000lb. The first B-36J flew in July 1953, and a total of 33 was built (14 of these being featherweight B-36J-IIIs).

The 'featherweight' B-36Js had all guns removed, (except those in the tail), observer blisters covered with flat windows, and the crew reduced to thirteen. The reduced weight allowed the 'featherweights' to operate at 47,000 — 50,000ft. By this time most of SAC's B-36 fleet was showing its age and in need of replacement. However, because of the unexpected delays in the deployment and operational readiness of the Boeing B-52s, the B-36s had to remain in use much longer than planned. It took time to transition crews to the B-52s, to certify them for nuclear alert, and practice launch under warning. Retaining the B-36s required much ingenuity and hard work by all SAC members

Replacement parts were salvaged from aircraft in long-term storage at Davis-Monthan AFB, Arizona, while Specialised Aircraft Maintenance Work (SAM-SAC) was performed at Convair San Diego to extend the bombers life. By the end of 1958, SAC had thirteen B-52 Bomb Wings, each with a complement of 45 to 50 Stratofortresses and by 1959, all the B-36 Peacemaker bomber fleet had been retired, replaced by the big Boeing.

No B-36s flew in combat, even with the Far East Air Force (FEAF) during the Korean War. By December 1950, SAC only had 38 B-36s and 20 RB-36s held back for atomic strike missions. Deciding not to risk its B-36s in Korean skies, SAC deployed five B-29 medium Bomb Groups to the FEAF. The B-36 were part of America's nuclear deterrent from November 1948 to February 1959, by which time SAC had a large force of B-47 Stratojets and B-52s, as well as the first generation of ICBMs.

Chapter 7   Convair B-58 Hustler

The shortest ever serving bomber to appear in the SAC inventory was the Convair B-58 Hustler. The basic concept of the B-58 was that of a tailless delta with an amazingly thin wing and no internal bomb-bay, the bomb-load being carried in a giant pod hung under the fuselage centre-line. A delta-winged bomber with an external ordnance load was a very unusual concept when development work began on the B-58 in the early 1950s, and the Convair engineering team at Fort Worth, Texas, produced numerous designs, including a number of full-scale mock-ups, before deciding on the final configuration of the B-58 Hustler.

So many new design concepts were introduced with the Hustler that at least a dozen could have gone wrong. What made the airplane 'work' was the four 7,076 kg (15,600lb) thrust afterburning General Electric J79-GE-5B single-spool turbojets, a new generation of power plant the availability of which was far from assured at the time the Hustler project began. The J79 engine was a giant leap forward in jet engine technology and it made the engine — always to be remembered for its highly visible clouds of black smoke it emitted and ear-shattering noise during take-off — about 40 per cent lighter than comparable engines.

Like other SAC bombers of the era, the B-58 defended itself using a tail gun, a 20-mm M61A1 "Gatling" gun operated similarly as on the B-47, by a forward crew member. Though it was unlikely the bomber was going to get into any skirmishes with Soviet MiGs as it was faster than most of those in Soviet Air Force (VVS) service at the time.

Having been designed and assembled in greater secrecy than usual, the first B-58 Hustler was rolled-out on 31 August 1956, and made a virtual perfect first flight on 11 November that year, flown by test pilot B A Erickson. A month later it became the first bomber to exceed Mach 1.0. Looking like a giant bat in the air, and while on the ground, appearing rather ungainly with its high, narrow track landing gear specifically designed to give clearance for its jettisonable under-fuselage MB-1 pod, combining weapons (nuclear or conventional), fuel, and reconnaissance equipment carriage, - the Hustler entered service with SAC on 15 August 1960.

In the end, only 116 Hustlers were built between 1956 and 1962, all being B-58A models except the eight airplanes which were converted to TB-58A (first flight 10 May 1960) trainer standard. One NB-58A was deployed as a flying test-bed for the J93-GE-3 engine later used by the cancelled supersonic (Mach 3.0) North American B-70 Valkyrie, the engine carried under the Hustler's fuselage.

A total of 108 series production Hustlers were delivered to SAC (in addition to the two prototypes and eleven airplanes were used for trials and development work). In its relatively short service career from 1960 to 1970, the type set numerous speed and altitude records.

Declared fully operational on 1 August 1960, they served with the 43rd Bomb Wing (BW) at Carswell AFB, Texas, and Little Rock AFB, Arkansas, and the 305th Bomb Wing at Bunker Hill AFB, Indiana (later Grissom AFB). The 43rd Bomb Wing being the first to receive the type.
The introduction of such an advanced new bomber, capable of speeds over Mach 2.0 required special training. Those crews on nuclear alert will never forget long hours of hanging around in a state of high readiness in the 'alert' barracks at the base, the "Hidden Hilton" at Little Rock and the "Mole Hole" at Bunker Hill.

The B-58 was sleek, eerie and an impressive airplane, looking more like an oversize fighter. But, it was not easy to maintain and less easy to fly. Though B-58 crews had considerable pride in their 'hot' aircraft, it demanded much from them. It was cramped, noisy, uncomfortable and crammed with complex items of equipment. It was also very expensive to operate, even in the free-spending early years of the Cold War, SAC calculated that one hour of flying time in the B-58 cost four times as much as an hour in the Boeing B-47 Stratojet.

On 23 March 1960, a B-58 set an endurance record of 18 hours 10 minutes, covering 11,000 miles and averaging 620 mph. On 11 January 1961 in Operation *Quick Step* a B-58 Hustler set three world payload records, flying over a 2,000 miles closed-circuit course at an average speed of 1,061.80 mph. On 13 January 1961, another B-58 averaged 1,284.73 mph over a 1,000 km closed-circuit with a 2,000 kg payload.

In an effort to show its new bomber to the world, on 26 May 1961, SAC flew a B-58 from New York to Paris in 3 hours 19 minutes. Later at the Paris Air Salon - two Hustlers crashed — although the following year the aircraft redeemed itself with more record-breaking flights. On 5 March 1962, a flight from Los Angeles to New York was accomplished in 2 hours 1 minute. The following year, on 16 October 1963, a B-58 undertook the world's longest supersonic flight when it travelled from Tokyo to London, a distance of 8,028 miles in 8 hours 35 minutes, at an average speed of 938 mph.
The Hustler's war-load weighed up to 8,823 kg (19,450lb) was carried inside the under-fuselage pod, and consisted of six types of nuclear bombs, including the B 43 and B 61 gravity weapons that were standard in the USAF's arsenal at the time.

Pentagon experts formed a steering group and spent six months studying a conventional mission for the B-58 — with the country deeply immersed in south-east Asia at the time — but ultimately never gave the Hustler any job other than to deliver nuclear bombs.

Pilots and crew of the Hustler had a kind of love-hate relationship with the bomber. They knew the were crammed inside one of the world's top-performing warplanes, assigned a Doomsday mission, and were expected not to kill themselves when the bomber was in its most unforgiving mode, especially when descending on its final approach. The aircraft had to be flown with great care and could be dangerously unforgiving. Ignoring the predefined ranges of angle of attack in take-off, landing and cruise could end in disaster. Loss of an engine at high speed could cause the aircraft to yaw drastically and rip itself to pieces. Loss of hydraulic control demanded an immediate bail out.

A total of twenty-six B-58s were lost in accidents, and the type had the unfortunate distinction of suffering fatal crashes twice at the Paris Air Show, once in 1961 and again in 1965.

Early production airplanes featured conventional ejection seats, but in 1962, after the deaths of aircrew in high-speed ejections, a new 'escape capsule' scheme was introduced that sealed each crew member into a clamshell capsule to improve his chances of survival in a supersonic ejection. The capsule would self-stabilise after ejection; had inflatable flotation devices for water landings; and had a survival kit, including a radio and even a survival rifle !

The B-58 Hustler was considered a 'dasher' it could cruise at Mach 0.91, climb to 15,240 metres (50,000ft) and descend to attack. The profile became too vulnerable after SAMs came into widespread use. The Hustler could be flown above 50,000ft but not officially without a pressure suit. In operational combat the bomber could be easily be taken above 18,288 metres (60,000ft).

Variants of the Hustler bomber that were never built included a proposal for a 'stretched' B-58B for SAC, a B-58C variant which would have had Pratt & Whitney J58 engines, the B-58D long-range, all-weather interceptor for the Air Defence Command (ADC) also powered by J58s, and a B-58E twin-engine version for Tactical Air Command (TAC). But, none of these came to fruition, as by 31 December 1969, after less than a decade of operational service, the last B-58 was retired from SAC. Viewed at the time it entered service as a dramatic advance over the Boeing B-52 Stratofortress, the B-58 Hustler ended up entering front-line service several years after the 'Buff' and ended its career decades before the big Boeing. Having never dropped a bomb in combat.

In truth SAC commander General Curtis E LeMay never liked the Hustler, and wanted to get rid of it beginning in about 1965 or so because he really wanted the North American B-70 Valkyrie that was still in the design stage at this time, and was going to be SAC's next great bomber. In any case the odds were stacked against the Hustler, it was expensive to operate, it was a complicated airplane, it didn't enjoy a good safety record, and it lacked low-level terrain-avoidance equipment, which limited its ability to get down low. But, if the proposed more advanced model had been produced with solid-state instruments it could have been the greatest bomber ever.

Chapter 8 General Dynamics FB-111A Aardvark

The General Dynamics FB-111A strategic bomber, based on the F-111D fighter-bomber design, made its first flight on 30 July 1967. It had a variable-geometry wing and was powered by two 20,350lb thrust Pratt & Whitney TF30-P-7 turbofan engines. Somewhat larger than the F-111D tactical fighter-bomber; length is 73ft 6in and wing-span 33ft 11in. Maximum take-off weight is 119,000lb. The FB-111A equipped two SAC bombardment wings, but were re-assigned to TAC as F-111Gs before some were retired and others were sold to Australia.

Although viewed by most as an 'interim' solution, SAC members who flew the FB-111A strike bomber were equally proud of their airplane as their colleagues who flew the much larger B-52s and B-1Bs.

The aircraft was based on the F-111 tactical fighter, that got off to a bad combat career in south-east Asia, that after extensive re-design and modification work, in 1972 returned to south-east Asia and redeemed itself.

The FB-111A filled a requirement for a supplemental bomber to augment the SAC force until a next-generation bomber (the Rockwell B-1B) could become operational. Designed as a nuclear strike aircraft, it could carry up to fifty 750lb bombs using both its internal bomb bay and six under-wing hard-points with multiple ejector racks (MERs), although the external load was impractical for a strategic mission. Total bomb-load was around 38,000lb or nearly double that of the F-111 tactical fighter variant. With a variable-geometry wing and strengthened landing gear, the FB-111A was as close to a strategic bomber as an airplane of its size could be…

The FB-111A force comprised two SAC wings, the 380th Bomb Wing at Plattsburgh AFB, New York, and the 509th at Pease AFB, New Hampshire. The FB-111A would have been only marginally effective operating from Stateside bases, but could have rapidly deployed to forward bases closer to its intended targets. The introduction of the Rockwell B-1B Lancer allowed the retirement of the FB-111A from the strategic role with SAC, airframes being converted to F-111G standard for tactical use with TAC. Force cutbacks following the end of the Cold War led to only 30 aircraft being converted and to the retirement of the type in 1994. Some of these airplanes were then sold on to Australia as spares ships and attrition replacements for the RAAF's F-111Cs that remain in use in 2007.

Chapter 9   Stealth Pioneers (Northrop XB-35 and XB-49)

John Northrop built his first flying-wing in 1929, the design offering a lower drag and therefore higher performance on given power. In July 1940, Northrop flew his N-1M with two small piston engines buried in the thick wing to drive pusher propellers, the performance of which did much to convince USAAF 'top brass' that a flying wing strategic bomber was feasible. Four 18.29 metre (60ft) span N-9M flying-wing demonstrators were built, the first of them flying in December 1942.

In November 1941, the USAAF had ordered two XB-35 bombers with contra-rotating pusher propeller units, and a further 13 service evaluation and test aircraft were ordered in early 1943 by way of eight YB-35s and five YB-35As. There were many problems to be resolved, especially with propellers and gearboxes, and the first XB-35 (serial 42-13603) did not fly until 25 June 1946. Exactly a year and a day later the second XB-35 serial 42-38323 took to the air, but with the Second World War ended the programme had lost its impetus. Nevertheless, considerable effort went into the development programme. But, by this time, the massive Convair B-36 was available and the new generation of Boeing jet bombers were on the horizon, so the contract for the 200 B-35A flying wing Northrop bombers was cancelled.

In 1941, still convinced of the merits of the design, Northrop proposed to the USAAF a further flying wing type with very long range and gained permission to convert two YB-35s for jet propulsion. These were revised with eight 1,814 kg (4,000lb) thrust Allison J45-A-5 turbojets replacing the XB-35s four 3,000hp Pratt & Whitney R-4360 radial piston engines. Designated YB-49 the type flew for the first time in October 1947. A third conversion flew in 1950 as the sole YB-49A with six 2,450 kg (5,600lb) thrust J35-A-21 engines, four buried in the wing roots and the other two located in under-wing pods. The YB-49 offered considerable performance, attaining a maximum speed of 837 km/h (520 mph) at 8,990 metres (29,500ft); a service ceiling of 10,975 metres (36,000ft) and range of 5,530 km (3,435 miles). In spite of this an production order for 30 B-49s was cancelled after the second YB-49 broke up in the air with the loss of all five crew, the more conventional piston-engined Convair B-36 being preferred.

The crew for the proposed B-35 long-range bomber was to have been nine: a pilot, a co-pilot, a bombardier, a navigator, an engineer, a radio operator and three gunners. Six relief crew members were to be carried for long-range missions. The crew nacelle was located at the centre of the wing and it was divided into three parts, exclusive of the tail-cone. The forward section housed the flight crew. The crew's quarters had provisions for relief flight crew bunks and the aft gunner's position. The pilot sat in a Plexiglass bubble to the left of the aircraft's centre-line. The co-pilot was seated to the right of and below the pilot's position, behind a large heavily braced window in the leading edge of the wing, which featured a view above and below.

The conventional flight instruments were arranged in a slightly unconventional manner in the cockpit. Flight instruments were on a vertical panel, between the pilot's position, while the radio equipment and propeller controls were on the pedestal, which separated the pilot's stations. One set of throttle controls was suspended from the top of the cabin between the pilot and co-pilot.

In the jet-propelled YB-49 the flight instruments had a more ergonomic look. The two overhead throttles, for the eight jet engines replaced the four piston engine controls. The central pedestal, which was cluttered because of the controls for the propellers and some radio controls, was considerably improved by their absence. The complete crew nacelle was pressurised and the crew were free to move about throughout the nacelle while the aircraft was in the air.

The flying-wing bombers were equipped with a low pressure, demand-type oxygen system with each crew member having access to oxygen equipment. The crew nacelle was heated, ventilated, defrosted and pressurised. In the YB-49 this was accomplished by using hot air, which came from the compressor section of the jet engine. There was a separate system on each side of the aircraft. The air for each system was ducted through a shut-off valve and an after-cooler, before it was brought to the crew compartment. The after-cooler drew its air from the bomb-bay and the cooling air was exhausted through an opening in the upper wing surface. Controls in the crew compartment, which were set manually, controlled the nacelle temperature. The range of the control was from 40 to 60 degrees. Compartment pressure was controlled by an automatic pressure regulator, which was installed aft of the turret structure of the crew's quarters.

The prototypes were constructed of a new aluminium developed by the Alcoa Company. When tested, this material was found to be considerably stronger than the previously used 24 ST material. Fuel was carried in bullet-proof and leak-proof fuel cells within the wing structure. In addition to the standard fuel tanks, additional fuel could be carried by placing auxiliary tanks in two of the aircraft's eight bomb-bays. Normal fuel capacity was 30,283 litres (8,000 US Imp Gals), but the XB-35 had a maximum fuel capacity of 68,137 litres (18,000 gals) giving a range of approximately 12,069 km (7,500 miles). There were four main tanks plus six auxiliary and four bomb-bay tanks.

Long-range armament was to include a 4,500 kg (10,000lb) bomb-load, divided among six small bays, which precluded the carriage of the early nuclear weapons. There were three bomb-bays in each wing. Each of the bays was equipped with a flexible segmented door that rolled onto drums at the aft end of the bays when opened.

In series B-35s there were to be seven power turrets for twenty 0.5-in machine-guns or 20mm cannons in three turrets on the centre-line and four turrets above and below the outer wings, the system pioneered on the Northrop P-61 night fighter. There were to be four manned sighting stations provided for the control of the turrets.

Maximum bomb-load for short-range missions of around 1,167 km (725 miles) would have been thirty-two 726 kg (1,600lb) bombs, for a total weight of 23,675 kg (52,193lb). No defensive armament was fitted to the prototype XB-35. For the turbojet-powered airplane the bomb-load was to be 4,536 kg (10,000lb) over a range of 4,500 km (2,800 miles) and no defensive armament was intended to be

Powered by four 18-cylinder P&W Wasp Major R-4360-17 outer and –21s inner, all of the XB-35s engines developed 3,000 hp each and were equipped with General Electric turbo-chargers. In the wing leading edges slits supplied the air needed by the four engines. All four were fitted with Hamilton-Standard constant-speed, full-feathering, dual-rotational, eight-bladed, contra-rotating propellers. The engines and their extended drive shafts were completely enclosed in the wings.

Much effort was needed to perfect the Flight Control System (FCS) and the bomber's response in all flight conditions. As for example bomb-aiming required accurate yaw control at high altitude, and the fin area for directional stability was provided by the propellers. It is of interest to note much time was spent studying yaw control at high altitude as the first aircraft (serial 42-10236673) was fitted with a six-bladed propeller unit on the No.1 engine and an eight-bladed unit on Nos. 2, 3 and 4.

Eventually, to improve stability at altitude, the second B-35 (42-38323) was fitted with single-rotation four-bladed propellers, with square-tipped hollow steel blades. This airplane first flew on 26 June 1947. Only one more B-35 was flown, the first of six YB models (serial 42-102366), flown on 15 May 1948. This also had single-rotation propellers.

The B-35s stood over 6 metres (20ft) tall on their tricycle undercarriage to ensure sufficient ground clearance for their props. All three undercarriage units retracted into the fuselage/wing to lay flat. An emergency release system was incorporated in the landing gear control system. If this was activated then the gear would remain down. Each main gear wheel was also equipped with dual spot-type brakes.

In the air the XB-35 was controlled by elevons, trim flaps and rudders. Roll was created by the elevons working in opposition. Pitch was achieved by the elevons working in unison. Aerodynamic trim was provided by small electrically-operated 'trim-flaps'. The rudders were split flaps located on the trailing edge, at the wing tips. They were operated one at a time and provided directional control. The split flaps also produced drag for speed control when they were operated together.

On the jet versions of the bomber, the vertical fins were installed on the wings upper surfaces to replace the aerodynamic stabilising effects of the four propellers and their associated shaft housings. Completing the control surfaces were the large split-flap landing flaps. These were located on the inboard portion of the wing. To delay stall, wing-tip slots were used in the wing's leading edge, near each tip. The slots were provided with hydraulically-actuated doors which automatically closed the openings for cruise flight and opened the slots for low-speed operations, or whenever the landing gear was extended. Hot air from the outboard engine heat exchangers was diverted through the leading edge of the outer wings for de-icing.

Having reverted to simpler propellers on the XB-35s it was found they were unable to convert all the engine power into thrust, especially at height, maximum speed falling from 629 to 587 km/h (391 to 365 mph). The USAF agreed with Northrop that the best solution was to fit turbojet engines.

Subsequently on 1 June 1945, the air force approved Northrop's proposal to complete two of the first five unfinished YB-35s with eight axial turbojets in the 17.79 kN (4,000lb) class, the powerplants selected, the General Electric TG-180, which gave rise to the Allison J35.

Conversion to jet propulsion went extremely smoothly, and even the inlets and ducts posed no problems. However, continued development resulted in only two YB-49s, these being converted YB-35s 2 and 3, serials 42-10367 and 42-102368 respectively. The first YB-49 taking off from Hawthorne on 21 October 1947, with the same flight crew as had flown the first XB-35 prototype just over a year earlier. The second YB-49 flew on 13 January 1948.

From the start these unique jet bombers performed outstandingly. Though the main incident of concern was the crash of the No.2 aircraft. It was subsequently established that the outer wings had separated during overload dive and pull-out tests at extreme forward centre of gravity. All aboard were killed, and the USAF pilot, Captain Glen Edwards, gave his name to Muroc, which was renamed Edwards AFB.

The accident happened on 5 June 1948, and five days later the USAF announced it was buying 30 RB-49A jet reconnaissance-bombers, the first to be built by Northrop and the other 29 made by Convair at Fort Worth. Northrop were also contracted to complete the remaining ten (of 13) YB-35s to a new RB-35B configuration, with six 24.91 kN (5,600lb) J35-21 jet engines, four in the wing and two in under-wing pods. This arrangement availing the carriage of extra fuel in the space provided by halving the volume of the internal engine ducts. But, by late 1948, the whole programme was becoming very complex. The eighth YB-35 was to be converted into the YRB-49A, with the RB-35B engine installation but with electronics and reconnaissance systems. The EB-35B was to have the same powerplant plus two Northrop-Hendy Turbodyne 10,400hp turboprops driving pusher propellers.

Finally out of all this planning only one actual airplane evolved, the YRB-49A. On 28 October 1949, almost all the other programmes were cancelled leaving only the YRB-49A serial 42-102376. This aircraft made a successful first flight on 4 May 1950. crewed by pilots Fred Bretcher and Dale Johnson, and with Frank Schroeder as engineer. On this first flight it was delivered from Hawthorne to Muroc (renamed Edwards), to begin intensive flight tests in the reconnaissance role. It was actually placed in storage at Ontario International Airport ten months later and was scrapped in October 1953.

Of the XB-35s, the first moved under its own power in a slow taxi test on 16 May 1946. These tests were followed by high-speed taxi tests, during which speeds of 185 km/h (115 mph) were attained. At 10.00am, on 25 June 1946, the first prototype took to the air for the first time with very few observers on hand — a company order had restricted the number of bystanders in the area due to concerns over safety and crowd control. Even John Northrop stayed in his office to comply with the company directive.

Tupolev Tu-4 Bull 01 with bomb load note above fuselage rear-facing machine-gun

As WW II drew to a close, the Japanese islands were pulverised by daily raids by huge formations of Boeing B-29 Superfortress long-range strategic bombers

Hiroshima on 5 August 1945. The atomic explosion impelled a mushroom cloud of smoke and debris to 60,000ft above the city.

The total devastation as wrecked by a thermo-nuclear weapon. Hiroshima was utter destruction for five square miles. In this area thousands of people were killed . Many more died from exposure to radiation, both at the time, and many thousands more over the succeeding years.

'Darkest Hour' B-52G of the 379th Bomb Wing prepares to roll for another long flight to the Gulf from RAF Fairford in the UK

A B-52G 'somewhere over the Gulf' while refuelling from a Boeing KC-135 en-route to it's target. 1,624 missions were flown by B-52G's and 72,000 weapons dropped during Gulf War I making a total of 25,700 tons of munitions which constituted 30% of all USAF bombs and 29% of all bombs dropped

SAC FB-111A strategic bomber prepared to 'start' engines with ground-crew members in attendance on the ramp

The FB-111A Aardvarks side-by –side seating prompted greater crew co-ordination compared to tandem seating. The left-hand seat is the pilot's equipped with head-up display (HUD). The right-hand seat is occupied by the weapon system operator (WSO) with displays for viewing the radar, Pave Tack or EOGB video

B-1B Lancer undergoing pre-flight checks

The four decoy ALE-50 installation can be seen fitted to the port rear fuselage of this Rockwell B-1B. There is a similar installation on the starboard side

The ALE-50 decoy installation 'scabbed on' the Rockwell B-1B Lancers rear fuselage—shown in close-up above—can just be seen in this photograph

Rockwell B-1B Flight Profiles:

Northrop Grumman B-2 manufacturing facility at Plant 42, Palmdale, California. Work in progress on prototype models AV-1 to AV-6

The B-2's birthplace was Plant 42 at Palmdale, Nevada where AV-2 to AV-10 can be seen taking shape. Wing leading edges have been covered to conceal the stealth technology

White paint was used as a bonding to which RAM (Radar Absorbent Material) was attached. The dark mats used to afford a degree of walkway protection for manufacturing personnel

The B-2 has two weapons bays mounted side-by-side in the lower centrebody, each fitted with a Boeing rotary launcher assembly to launch it's GPS-guided 227kg (500lb) JDAM and JASSM

Despite it's complexity, the B-2 Spirit is flown by two crew members, although a third seat is provided for an additional member. Note the fighter-type control column. The B-2s crew consist of a commander and a pilot

Flying low over the Nevada desert near Edwards AFB, California, this shot of the aircraft clearly shows the shock wave that surrounds it when flying at high Mach.

The flight crew consisted of Max Stanley, test pilot; Charles Fred Bretcher, co-pilot; and Orva Douglas, flight engineer. After an uneventful flight over the Sierra Madre, the flying-wing landed at Muroc, 44 minutes after it had taken off. The flight being completely uneventful except for erratic operation of a propeller governor.

Problems with the Hamilton-Standard propeller governors continued for sometime. Propellers would 'hunt' around a constant-speed setting and 'creep' in fixed pitch during air tests. In addition there was evidence the massive contra-rotating propellers were operating under stress, that lead to a restriction of 80 hours operating time before replacement, due to the danger of disintegration due to fatigue.

The second XB-35, serial 42-38323, arrived at Muroc, after another uneventful first flight on 26 June 1947. However, even before the first flight of these unique flying-wing bombers, there was a strong possibility the more conventional pusher Convair XB-36 would be SAC's new piston-engined long-range strategic bomber. In an attempt to keep the project alive, Northrop recommended that two YB-35s be completed as turbojet YB-49s. The USAF also decided to edge its bets and instructed Northrop to continue with the production of six YB-35s, as they would have greater range and be capable of carrying a greater bomb-load. When completed they were to be equipped with more up-to-date navigation and weapons systems and be re-designated YB-35As. One of the YB-35s was to have been handed over to the US Navy for evaluation, but this plan was cancelled. The proposed designation for this aircraft was XB2T-1.

As testing of the first prototype XB-35 progressed, the fledgling television industry became a means of advancing aircraft testing. The No 1 test aircraft was equipped with a Navy type television camera system to pick up readings on the flight instrument panel. This was done on the airplanes first, second and third flights. The TV pictures were transmitted to the P-61 chase plane. In the Northrop P-61 night fighter a television set located at the radar operator's station displayed the readings on the screen, while a motion picture camera, facing the TV set recorded the data on film.

As the test programme continued, all eyes fell on the jet-powered YB-49 serial 42-102367, that was displayed to the public for the first time on 29 September 1947. It undertook its first taxi test on 20 October 1947, and made its maiden flight the next day, flown out of Hawthorne by the same crew as had flown the XB-35. The flight was once again, uneventful. Flight time from Hawthorne to Muroc was just 32 minutes, and the only problem encountered was slowing the bomber to land, as no flaps were used. Subsequently, YB-49 serial 42-102378 was also delivered to Muroc on 13 January 1948. The YB-49s were more reliable airplanes than were the XB-35s, but instead of prop and gearbox problems, it had auxiliary power unit electrical problems and its J35 turbojets exhibited poor reliability. Early on in the jets test programme, the bomber was found to be unacceptably unstable as a bomber platform due to an inadequate rate of yaw oscillation damping.

At the same time as the YB-49s were entering their test programme, the piston-engined XB-35s were still experiencing problems with their contra-rotating propellers. As before, the problems centred on the propeller governor and in the gearbox. Northrop and its sub-contractors were desperate to find a solution, but in the end, it was decided the reduced performance of the aircraft fitted with the single rotation propellers would have to be accepted if the XB-35 was to be a success. Therefore, four-bladed, single-rotation propellers were fitted to two XB-35s and the one YB-35 built serial 42-102366. These propellers had a larger diameter blade than did the original propellers, but they were still unable to absorb the full power of the P&W Wasp Major piston engines.

By 15 May, the third B-35, YB serial 42-102366 had been flown to Muroc, and all three B-35s were equipped with single rotation propellers. On the 13 January 1948, the first flight of the second YB-49 jet serial 42-102368, took place, the aircraft piloted by Major R L Cardenas.

Unfortunately six months later this airplane crashed while on trials out of sight of the observers. Over the Antelope Valley test range it had shed its two outer wing sections, leaving the main centre section to crash into the desert. As already related, all the crew were killed.

Despite the crash, after two years of testing, the USAF was convinced that the YB-49 jet bomber was a world-beater, at the time acknowledged as the longest legged jet in the world. Indeed just five days after the crash, as a show of confidence in the airplane the USAF placed an order for 30 RB-49As to fill a requirement for a long-range strategic reconnaissance bomber. When the contract was signed all the indications were this unusual flying-wing design would enter USAF service. But, in truth the programmes and the airplanes days were already numbered.

At the same time, the test programme and production planning continued in respect of the older B-35, but recurring problems with vibration associated with the single rotation propellers, coupled with metal fatigue, were causing premature failures of the engine cooling fans and this was giving rise to grave doubts as to the deployment of the aircraft as a strategic bombing platform. In addition there were serious maintenance problems associated with the intricate exhaust system of the R-4360 Wasp Major engines.

In the end, none of the proposed RB-49A jets were ever produced. The type was a victim of the constantly changing requirements and severe post-war budgetary constraints. Along with the cancellations of the 30 RB-49As, a planned conversion of ten YB-35s to a new turbojet-powered configuration, designated RB-35B, announced in November 1948, was also cancelled. These cancellations were designed to release around $300 million into the Convair B-36/RB-36 programme, as well as pay for the upgrade of SAC Boeing piston-engined B-50s.

Nevertheless, the USAF continued to keep Northrop's hopes of saving the flying-wing design by suggesting a whole series of alternative roles for the YB-35 airframes. These hopes were kept alive by the No 1 YB-49 jet in February 1949, when the aircraft flew from Edwards AFB, California to Andrews AFB, outside Washington, DC, a distance of 3,630 km (2,258 miles), in four hours 25 minutes, at an average speed of 822 km/h (511 mph).

In another spectacular performance the YB-49 flew a long-range test flight, which took place on 26 April 1948. The airplane remained aloft for 9.5 hours, of which 6.5 hours were flown at an altitude of 12,200 metres (40,000ft). The flight crew on this flight being the original Northrop trio of Max Stanley, Fred Bretcher and O H Douglas, plus USAF Captain Jay Wethe and Northrop Flight Engineer Don Swift.

Northrop in turn also submitted several variations of the design in a hope to save the programme. A turboprop-engined bomber was proposed (in 2004, the RAF announced it was evaluating the Airbus Military A400M turboprop strategic transport — still to fly in 2006 — as a long-range strategic bomber, cruise missile carrier), along with an escort fighter, a 'cargo pack', and a boundary layer control flying-wing.

The most unusual of the Northrop suggestions did actual make it into hardware, this was the EB-35. The EB-35B was to be a test-bed for the XT-37T Turbodyne, a gas turbine powerplant. The aircraft to have, in addition to its six J35 engines a T-37 Turbodyne engine generating 10,000hp. Six other YB-35s were earmarked for conversion to a six-turbojet set-up, with again, four of the engines buried in the wing, with two engines hung on pylons under it. These six were designated YB-35Bs. They were to have been used as advanced test platforms for flying-wing type aircraft. Of the total number contracted for under the designations EB-35B and YB-35B, two aircraft were started and completed, but neither was destined to fly.

Another nail in the coffin of the YB-49 jet, occurred in November 1948, when Major Robert L Cardenas stated, for the record, that the YB-49 was "extremely unstable and very difficult to fly on a bombing mission — because of continual yawing and pitching which was evident upon application of the rudders."

Colonel Albert Boyes, Chief, of the Flight Test Division, agreed wholeheartedly with that statement. On 16 November 1948, Air Material Command reported that the YB-49 under manual bombing testing, had, "marginal directional stability". On 29 December 1948, a board of senior officers recommended cancellation of the thirty RB-49s. On 11 January 1949, Air Material Command ordered Northrop to stop work on all phases of the reconnaissance programme with the exception of one airplane to be completed as an YRB-49A.

This airplane would be equipped with autopilot, an ARQ-24 radar and suitable camera installations. Also a flash bomb-bay was to be incorporated to carry six flash bombs. The bomb-bay was to be large enough to take the new bombs under development and consideration at the time. YRB-49A serial 42-102376 was powered by six Allison J35-A-19 engines, which were rated at 24.9 kN (5,600lb) s. t. each. The engine installation was as for the proposed YB-35B.

In February 1949, the decision was taken to scrap the two XB-35s serials 42-13603 and 42-38323 and the YB-35 serial 42-102366, all the P&W Wasp Major piston-engined aircraft.

Tests with the YB-49, with an E-7 autopilot installed, were carried out in May 1949, piloted by Max Stanley, and later during April and June 1949, the aircraft was evaluated by Major Russ Schluh, who had replaced Major Cardenas as project officer. Max Stanley had stated, that the USAF had "declared the airplane suitable for its mission", but Major Schluh declared this simply was not so.

In November 1949, all planned conversions of YB-35s were ordered to be cancelled and cut up. The sole exception was the one airframe earmarked for conversion to YRB-49A status. The ordered destruction of the other airframes began on 15 March 1950.

The 1950s flying-wing era, was dealt another blow on 15 March 1950, when the No 1 YB-49 was destroyed in a taxi accident at Edwards AFB, a little over a year after it completed its record flight from California to Maryland. During this same period, the sole YRB-49A was completed. It was equipped with the latest long-range photographic reconnaissance equipment. This one-and-only YRB-49A serial 42-102376, made its maiden flight from Hawthorne to Edwards on 4 May 1950. Early in 1951, it was flown to the Northrop facilities at Ontario International Airport, California, where it was placed in dead storage, in October 1953, and subsequently the USAF ordered this last example of John Northrop's 1950s flying-wing designs to the scrap yard.

The decision to finally abandon the all-jet flying-wing machines at this time, was based on the premise that the eight-jet version would not be available until January 1950 and would have an inadequate operating radius; the six-jet model, the YRB-49A, planned for 1951, would be slower than the Boeing B-47 Stratojet; the Turbodyne-equipped version would not be available until 1953, putting it into competition with the superior all-jet Boeing B-52 Stratofortress.

The Northrop flying-wings were simply overwhelmed by the performance and capabilities of Boeing's more conventional jet bomber designs. Although they were the largest and most successful all-wing designs of the era. No aircraft before or since has come close to the all-wing perfection of that that was the XB-35, YB-49 and YRB-49A, except perhaps the USAF's B-2 Spirit stealth bomber, also a Northrop design.

With the B-2 all John Northrop's work of early years was vindicated and has embodied the USAF with probably the most lethal manned aircraft in the world.

Chapter 10   Northrop Grumman B-2A Spirit 'Stealth' bomber

Not unexpectedly, the Northrop B-2 was developed amid tight security and secrecy, as one of America's so-called 'Black Programmes', so that it was not until the bombers roll-out, on 22 November 1988, that the airplane was seen in public, and then only from a closely controlled distance. All the new type's development expenditure had to be carefully hidden, and the programme was known only to a handful of Northrop and Boeing insiders, as well as some senior USAF officers and selected members of the Senate and House special committees. The bombers cover was finally blown on 20 April 1988, when the USAF released a very shaky artists impression of the airplane that did not show many of its interesting features. Even at the official roll-out on 22 November 1988, Northrop carefully managed the ceremony to hide details of the aircraft's wing design and the assembled guests had only a limited view of the aircraft. However, a major aviation periodical flew a light plane over the ceremony and the on-board photographer recorded the B-2's planform with great clarity. Subsequently, the prototype (AV-1, serial 82-1066) made its first flight on 17 July 1989, after which the aircraft entered into a 3,600 hour flight test programme, which included its first weapon drop during April 1992.

Following the first flight, the bomber emerged almost completely from the 'black' world, with various factions releasing information to either support further development and production of the airplane or call for its cancellation, to avoid the additional massive cost of the programme to the taxpayer. Of tailless flying-wing design (not a new concept for Northrop who investigated the design in the late 1940s - early 1950s — related in the previous chapter), using a three-dimensional computer-aided design and manufacturing system to create the aircraft's unique 'blended wing/double-W shape, the B-2 is powered by four General Electric F118-GE-100 84.5-kN (19,000lb) s. t. non-afterburning turbofans which give it almost the same thrust-to-weight ratio as the Rockwell B-1B, yet at the same time is extremely quiet, due to the aircrafts unique exhausts, which suppress noise and its infra-red signature. The B-2 can thus if necessary, operate from runways intended for civil airliners, in the Boeing B.727 class and can carry a payload of up to sixteen B 61 or B 83 nuclear bombs, and AGM-129 Advanced cruise missile's on rotary launchers inside its side-by-side weapons bays. Alternatively the aircraft can carry up to eighty Mk 82 1,000lb bombs, or sixteen laser– or TV-guided 2,000lb bombs, over a range of up to 12,230 km (7,600 miles).

Seven B-2s were used for development test work with the Combined Test Force (CTF) at Edwards AFB, California. Air Vehicle (AV) 1 was subjected to low-observable and initial-performance flight tests in February 1993, and was then placed in flyable storage at USAF Plant 42 in Palmdale, California.

AVs 2 to 6 were fully active in the flight test programme in 1994. AV 2 assigned to performance and high-angle-of-attack testing; AV 3 was used for testing of the Hughes APQ-181 radar and the defensive avionics, and for operational test and evaluation; AV 4 for armament testing and for the investigation of icing and rain effects. AV 5 was involved in a programme for defensive-avionics testing, as well as additional work on detectability and survivability; and AV 6 was used for testing navigation, radar and armament systems.

USAF B-2 Spirit

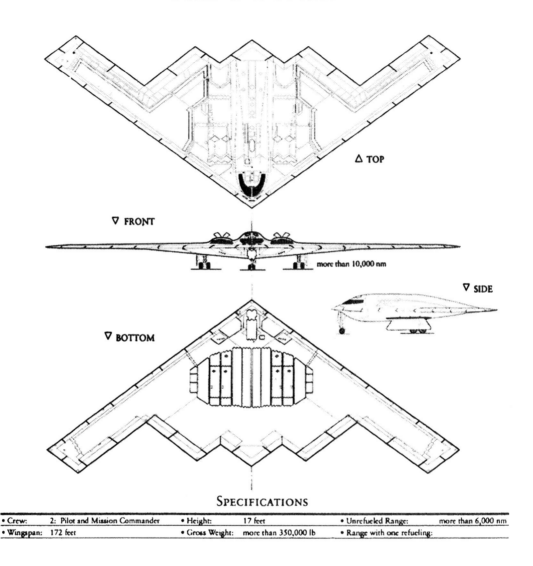

△ TOP

▽ FRONT

more than 10,000 nm

▽ SIDE

▽ BOTTOM

Specifications

• Crew:	2: Pilot and Mission Commander	• Height:	17 feet	• Unrefueled Range:	more than 6,000 nm
• Wingspan:	172 feet	• Gross Weight:	more than 350,000 lb	• Range with one refueling:	

"Nothing so well represented the air Force capability to conduct global attacks in the air war over Serbia as our B-2s delivering precision-guided munitions via 29-hour missions from Missouri to Yugoslavia and back". "The combination of on-board systems and GPS guidance on the B-2 proved even more accurate than planners had expected. This meant the B-2 could precisely engage multiple targets per sortie, destroying a disproportionate share of total targets in some of the most heavily defended areas of the conflict"

General Marvin R. Esmond USAF Deputy Chief of Staff. Testimony to the Senate 19 October 1999

AV 7 was assigned to the flight test programme for four months in 1993 and later underwent electro-magnetic interference and electronic-countermeasures testing while at Plant 42. It was then returned to Northrop for conversion to initial-production (Block 10) configuration, before being delivered to the first USAF B-2 operational unit, the 509th Bomb Wing (BW) at Whiteman AFB, Missouri, on 17 December 1993. Three additional aircraft were delivered by late 1994. Additional series production aircraft entered the operational test and evaluation programme (OT&E) for very short periods at times. Once all 20 aircraft had been delivered and the 16 operational machines divided between the 393rd and 750th Bomb Squadrons, only one aircraft was assigned for test purposes.

Much of the CTF's work involved addressing problems which showed up either during initial operations at Whiteman, or during the test programme itself. One of the first to appear after the types initial entry into the flight test programme, was the abnormal number of false alarms generated by the on-board test system (OBTS). Alarms were sometimes not discovered to be false until unnecessary tests and maintenance work had been carried out. Many of these arose as a result of OBTS problems, but once these had been sorted out, by the time 1,900 flight hours had been accumulated, the mean time between failure (MTBF) and the need for rectification stood at 63.5 hours, compared to the specification requirement of 67.9 hours, although these figures were from the test fleet and did not include data from the three operational B-2s at Whiteman AFB.

In addition an aft-deck cracking problem, recognised early in the bomber's development, was the main reason for the excessive failure rate at the start of the test programme. A new aft-deck was incorporated in series aircraft AV 14.

Other problems which affected the bombers reliability and maintainability included the freezing of water in the environmental-control system — a problem that was discovered during climatic testing at Elgin AFB, Florida.

Work around procedures, put in place before the first operational aircraft were delivered, proved to be quite effective, while permanent fixes were incorporated by 1995, in time for the hot– and cold–weather testing deployments.

Low-observable, or stealth, features are of course the major distinguishing features of the B-2 Spirit and as with the F-117 Night Hawk, it was discovered even the smallest error in manufacturing or assembly could severely affect the aircraft's stealthiness. One of these manufacturing errors, the incorrect application of ceramic coating on the engine tailpipes, caused the B-2 to fail one of 480 low-observable tests in early 1994.

Problems with tailpipes were discovered during production acceptance flights from Plant 42. At that time the CTF did not have an airplane capable of assisting with the definition and verification work. This was done on production aircraft from Plant 42. Following fitment of new tailpipes in late September 1994, to CTF aircraft AV 5 the types radar signature was re-validated, to ensure the bombers stealth parameters were maintained. Tests in late 1993, examined 272 different radar cross-section values and revealed that, in general, the bomber was slightly more stealthy than had been expected.

In late-1994, testing of the defensive-avionics suite had just begun, the specifications of which are a closely guarded secret, but it is known that it incorporates the Northrop Grumman ZSR-63 system. It is believed that the system actively emits radar waves to cancel incoming radar energy, working in a similar manner to an active noise-cancellation system.

Testing of the offensive-avionics suite, which is centred around the Hughes APQ-181 radar, had not at this time been completed, although testing of several modes of the radar had.
The low-probability-of-intercept J-band covert-strike radar has twenty-one modes. At the CTF it was believed there was a problem with the terrain-following mode, but neither Hughes or the USAF ever confirmed this.

One important task of the APQ-181 is to support the Global Positioning System (GPS) - Aided Targeting System (GATS), using ground imagery produced in synthetic-aperture-radar (SAR) mode. The GATS was developed by Hughes to enhance the B-2s conventional-weapons delivery accuracy, from 30 metres to within 6 metres. It combines GPS position data and SAR target imagery to give the bomber's stores-management system more precise weapon-aiming data for use with the Joint Direct Attack Munition (JDAM).

A limited GATS and JDAM 1 capability was built into the second series run of nine Block 20 aircraft, scheduled for delivery in 1996/97. GATS radar tests, were performed using a limited number of Northrop Grumman/Hughes GPS-aided munitions (GAMs).

Initial Block 10 aircraft were equipped to drop B 83 nuclear bombs or 900 kg Mk 84 unguided conventional bombs, while later Block 20 B-2s were also capable of launching the Northrop Grumman AGM-170 Tri-Service Stand-Off Attack Missile and the JDAM 1. Block 20 aircraft also carried B 61 nuclear bombs. Block 30 standard aircraft carry Mk 82 (225 kg) bombs, Mk 62 sea mines and cluster bombs. All 20 operational aircraft were to Block 30 standard by the year 2000.

The B-2 is reported to be pleasant and easy to handle in flight and through the full operational centre-of-gravity positions in flight, and varying airspeed/Mach-numbers and gross-weight combinations. Load testing to 100% of flight loads, was completed in July 1994, but additional ground-related tests were planned. At this time some analysis work, heavyweight take-offs and landings and brake testing remained before the full operating envelopes could be released to Air Combat Command.

The twenty-one B-2s built give the USAF Air Combat Command (ACC) an almost unstoppable, undetectable bomber capable of finding and attacking even mobile targets with impunity. In spite of the small number available (that in no way detracts from its capability and strike power) many claim the massive investment was worthwhile as the bomber was mostly responsible even before it entered service of ending the Cold War by bankrupting Russia's economy in their endeavours to develop a defence against it.

The entire force of 21 B-2 Spirit stealth bombers (only 16 operational at one time, with one used for tests) belong to the 509th Bomb Wing at Whiteman Air Force base, Missouri. Flown for the first time operationally over Kosovo in 1999, during Operation *Allied Force*, when it logged forty-five combat sorties flying non-stop to the Balkans from the United States. The unfortunate bombing of the Chinese Embassy in Belgrade by a B-2, was a disastrous US intelligence failure, rather than the fault of the aircraft or the crew flying it. Otherwise the bomber performed superbly.

The B-2 is ACC's premier bomber with a SIOP mission, meaning that it would be assigned to US Strategic Command (USSTRATCOM, or Stratcom for short) in wartime. It is the only American manned aircraft that could operate over hostile territory during an atomic war — the B-52 Stratofortress considered a stand-off platform in its SIOP role.

The B-2 Spirit can carry the standard B61-7, B61-11, and B83 Mod 0 gravity nuclear bombs. Although the practice of keeping bombers on nuclear 'alert' ended in 1991, a handful are kept 'on a short leash', not quite ready to launch, but almost. The exact status, including the time it would take to launch them with an atomic war-load, is not known.

As a conventional war-fighting tool the B-2 is a 'Silver Bullet' and was used in this role in 2003 when despatched to Iraq, to 'kill' Saddam Hussein, believed to be hiding in a remote farmhouse near Baghdad, to end Gulf War II before it began !

The 509th BW is dedicated to missions of high importance and which only the B-2 can perform. It can operate directly to anywhere in the world from the homeland, thereby negating any need for landing and over-flight permission from some other country.

Like the B-1B, the B-2 suffered early maintenance and logistics problems. Critics said, it would lose its radar-evading stealth qualities if left out in the rain. It is true that the radar-absorbent coating on the aircraft was vulnerable to moisture in its early version, but this was later greatly improved.
There is now no dispute that the B-2 is indeed stealthy, but its critics argue that any warplane must emit tell-tale radiation if interrogated during a mission, especially during the critical phase when enemy territory is being penetrated. The B-2's AN/APQ-181 radar (known as the radar sub-system or RSS) is optimised to emit the least energy necessary to do the job, and is known as the Low-Probability-of-Intercept (LPI) unit. The bomber's defensive aids sub-system, is highly classified, what is known is the most important element is the APR-50 unit, also called the ZSR-63 designed to detect, classify, identify and locate hostile systems that emit radio-frequency (RF) energy.

All 21 B-2s are now operational (includes productionised AV-1 prototype) to Block 30 standard. In the conventional role the bomber is cleared to carry JDAM munitions, CBU-87 cluster bombs, mines, and other specialised ordnance, in addition to the standard free-fall bombs on the USAF inventory.

A crew of two flies the bomber, although there is room for a third crew member. The aircraft commander, in the left seat, also performs the duties of the Weapons Systems Operator (WSO) and is responsible for targeting and weapon release. The interior of the airplane is spacious for a two-person crew, with room to lay out a li-low for 'cat-naps' during the 33-hour missions to Europe and back during Operation *Allied Force*. The pilots sit on standard ACES II ejection seats. Maximum speed is around 545 knots (1,010 km/h) above 12,200 metres (40,000ft). Indeed, any 21st century interceptor pilot that might find the stealth bomber en-route a hostile mission should have no problem engaging and despatching it. A flying-wing with a span of 52.43 metres or 172 ft, it presents a fairly easy target for modern air-to-air missiles. But, you have to find it first !

The first full-scale development B-2 made its inaugural flight at Air Force Plant 42, Palmdale, California, at 06.36 hours on 17 July 1989. With Northrop's chief test pilot Bruce J Hinds, and Air Force test pilot Lieutenant Colonel Richard S Couch at the controls the aircraft landed at Edwards AFB. The landing gear remained extended throughout the flight.

On 30th September 1990, the 509th Bombardment Group moved from Pease AFB, New Hampshire, to Whiteman AFB, Missouri, to begin planning to receive the new Northrop B-2 Spirit stealth bomber. While the 509th waited for the arrival of the new bomber, the USAF deactivated the Strategic Air Command (SAC) on 1 June 1992 and its assets and units were assimilated into the newly created Air Combat Command (ACC). On 20th July the Wing accepted its first aircraft in three years, a Northrop T-38 Talon trainer wearing a paint scheme similar to that of a B-2. Then on 17 December 1993, the first operational B-2 named the *Spirit of Missouri* arrived at Whitemen AFB. By May 1995, the 509th had received five more B-2s — appropriately named *Spirit of California, Spirit of Texas, Spirit of Washington, Spirit of Kansas* and *Spirit of South Carolina*. With two more aircraft scheduled for delivery by the year's end, to build an eventual inventory of 20 aircraft. As of May the 509th's fleet of B-2s had flown over 850 flying hours, while maintaining a sortie success rate of over 90 per cent.

The B-2 is without doubt one of the most unique airplanes ever to enter service with the USAF. In flight the tailless bomber appears deceptively small — but its has a 172ft wing-span, only 13ft less than the Boeing B-52, while being 69ft long, about six feet longer than the F-15 Eagle interceptor. Its four General Electric F-118-GE-100 engines produce a total of 69,200lbs of thrust to lift its 336,500lbs take-off weight into the skies to propel it at around 550 mph. For conventional bombing missions, the Spirit can carry up to sixteen Mk 84 2,000lb bombs, thirty-six cluster bomb units, or eighty Mk 82 500lb bombs up to 6,000 nautical miles without refuelling (although with just one in-flight refuelling it can strike anywhere in the world). It can of course, also carry nuclear weapons.

The B-2 incorporates the latest low-observable technologies to dramatically reduce its infra-red, acoustic, electromagnetic, radar, and even visual signatures. These technologies include state-of-the-art composite materials, special low-observable coatings, and the low profile of its all-flying wing design. Even the engine inlets and exhausts are carefully blended into the top of the wing. Every angle and curve on its exterior surface has been carefully crafted with stealth in mind.

The two combat squadrons at Whiteman AFB are the 393rd and the 325th BS. Both are fully operational and 'ready to go to war, both with conventional or nuclear weapons.' The training squadron is the 394th Combat Training Squadron, that runs the training school and takes care of the wing's fleet of 13 Northrop T-38 Talon supersonic companion trainers. The Talons maintained under a contract with Lockheed Martin Corporation. A full-motion-base flight simulator with full visual system, provides ground-based training. The 509th pilots routinely fly a mission rehearsal in the simulator the day before a B-2 mission to familiarise themselves with the scenario and to maximise their in-flight training.

The aircraft requires a crew of two, compared to the B-52's five-man crew and the B-1B's crew of four. Both of the B-2 crew members are rated pilots, the right seat pilot designated as the Mission Commander (MC) and the other designated as pilot. It is understood the pilot flies the bomber and the MC runs the systems and is in control of the mission, while both pilots share safety of flight decisions. The 509th Wing's concept of operations calls for an aircrew-to-aircraft ratio of 1.2-to-1. Selection for B-2 aircrew duty requires either 1,500 flying hours in bombers plus instructor pilot status or 1,000 hours in fighter aircraft.

After nine months of training, the 509th achieved a major milestone on 20 September 1994, by flying the *Spirit of California* on a seven-hour mission from Whiteman AFB to Utah Test and Training Range near Salt Lake City, Utah, and manually dropping two inert Mk 84 2,000lb bombs from an altitude of 30,000ft. The mission serving to exercise the Wing's mission planning process as well as the weapons load and aircraft preparation, that resulted in the successful release on time and on target.

In 1995, the Wings B-2s participated in the types first *Red Flag* exercise at Nellis AFB, Nevada, flying eight sorties between 21st January and 18th February. On the B-2's fifth *Red Flag* sortie, it dropped a pair of live 2,000lb Mk 84 bombs — the first live bomb drops and the first night *Red Flag* sortie by the bomber. According to air force officials, the B-2s scored ten targets hit for ten weapons released.

The *Red Flag* exercises, typically involving up to 100 aircraft (that includes a number from overseas air force's, such as RAF IDS Tornados etc.), 300 aircrew members, and over 1,000 support personnel, simulate combat scenarios for the US Air Force and Navy, as well as the air forces of its coalition partners.

Although the USAF is satisfied with its 21-aircraft B-2 inventory, several Congressman have been pushing for more to be procured. Northrop Grumman has offered to build more at a per-aircraft price of $570-630 million (£345-380 million). While air force chiefs have stressed the Air Force could not sacrifice other major programmes to build more B-2s, its enthusiasts, on occasion, continue to lobby for additional airplanes to be added to the stealth bomber fleet.

The Value of Stealth

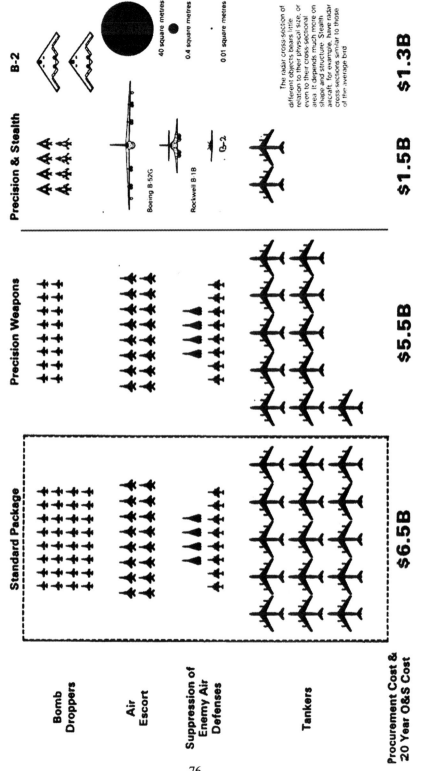

76.

The B-2 Spirit stealth bomber was declared operational by the USAF in 1997, with delivery of the 13th of the twenty-one airplanes built. It was used operationally for the first time during the 1999 Kosovo War and has subsequently operated over Afghanistan and Iraq in the war against terror. The raids launched from the airplanes home base of Whiteman AFB, Missouri in the United States. Although in 2003 the B-2 was forward deployed for the first time to conduct bombing missions over Iraq, sharing ramp space at Diego Garcia with ACC B-52s, B-1Bs and tanker aircraft. The B-2s dropping GPS-guided munitions, mostly JDAMS.

Development of the Northrop (Boeing) B-2 Spirit stealth flying-wing bomber started in 1978. Final development contracts were awarded to Northrop in November, 1981, for an ASPA (Advanced Strategic Penetrating Aircraft). The USAF wanted 113 B-2s to include the first six development aircraft, at an estimated cost of $36.6 billion. But the development of this strategic long-range heavy-bomber with low observable technology and all altitude capability permitting the penetration of the most sophisticated air defences was a gigantic task. 24,000 hours were spent on wind tunnel testing, 16,000 hours of engineering development testing, 42,000 hours for reliability testing, 122,000 hours for computer systems testing and 291,000 hours for flight qualification tests.

The B-2 programme combined revolutionary aerospace technologies and equally unprecedented design, development and manufacturing systems and processes to create the worlds most advanced bomber. Manufacturing time for the first prototype took 3,546 million man hours of which Northrop's portion amounted to 1.79 million. Northrop produced the forward centre section, the cockpit, outer-wing panels and of course final assembly. Boeing at Wichita produced the aft centre section in titanium, the huge outer-wing assemblies, fuel system, weapon delivery systems and landing gear. LTV at Grand Prairie; intermediate fuselage sections, aluminium and titanium structures and composites for other parts. Four General Electric F118-GE-110 non-after burning turbo-fans were mounted in pairs in the wings each side of the weapons-bay. The first aircraft (AV-1/ B2 -1066) was rolled out from USAF Plant 42 at Palmdale on the 22 November, 1988, making its first flight and delivery to Edwards AFB (2 hours and 20 minutes) on the 17 July 1989.

By the time of the first flight the overall cost of the programme had increased by 20%. In early 1990, the program cost was already calculated at $44,400 million. The collapse of the Soviet Union and the end of the Cold War and continually escalating costs forced the USAF into accepting a reduction to the procurement programme to 75 airplanes. Strategic Air Command (now Air Combat Command) originally wanted 165 airplanes.

Six aircraft were assigned to testing trials. The first four prototypes were accepted by the USAF between 1989-1992; one a year. The fifth flew on the 5 October, 1992, and the sixth aircraft on the 2 February, 1993, for avionics and weapons testing. As assembly experience was gained total production man-hours were reduced from 2,571 million man hours taken for the third aircraft to 2,156 million hours for the sixth. For the 11th projected production man hours was now 'only' 1,149 million man hours. Many hours were required for acceptance testing, 67,000 and a further 6,000 hours of flight tests and mission simulator time. A total of 897 days were consumed by ground checks and tests of the first prototype. More than two years !

Early in 1995, the USAF were obliged to accept a further reduction to the program. To only 21 airplanes at a fly-a-way cost of $837.5 million per aircraft. The first entering USAF service in 1996. Block 10 aircraft were upgraded to Block 20 standard commencing 1996. Later, all except one test airplane (later upgraded to Block-30 plus) based at Edwards AFB, California were upgraded to a common more capable Block 30 configuration the work completed in early 2001.

Northrop Grumman remained busy for a number of years at Palmdale and Pico River completing these tasks. Follow-on procurement has not been entirely ruled out but now seems unlikely. Northrop Grumman and Raytheon are developing a Block 40 upgrade package. Upgrading the APQ-181 radar with AESA that will improve bombing accuracy and change its Ku-band frequency to avoid interference with commercial signals from 2007. The all-new AESA would be fitted to the current radar. Northrop Grumman is hoping that funds be allocated in 2005 for other incremental enhancements, which could include updating computer software and processors, adding fibre-optic databuses, an auto-throttle and new cockpit displays. It has already been agreed to incorporate Link 16 datalink, integrating the 227kg (500lb) JDAM and JASSM. The B-2 has two weapons bays mounted side-by-side in the lower centrebody, each fitted with a Boeing rotary launcher assembly.

Other improvements would include removal of the 1980s-vintage avionics for a greatly enhanced capability commercial off-the-shelf (as is now common practice in the 21st century — with respect to a number of avionic upgrades) equipment and digital engine control.

Addendum

The USAF's entire fleet of Boeing B-2 Spirit stealth bombers were grounded after one of the aircraft crashed shortly after take-off from Andersen Air Force base, Guam, on 23 February 2008. B-2s normally based at Whiteman AFB, Missouri had been deployed to the Pacific area to maintain the US military presence in the Asia-Pacific region and deter potential enemies from taking surprise military action while other American forces are diverted to fighting in the Middle East. The loss of the aircraft reduces the total B-2 inventory to just twenty aircraft. Fortunately both crew members managed to eject safely before the crash, which occurred at 10.40a.m. on the island situated 3,700 miles south-west of Hawaii

Chapter 11 Rockwell B-1B Lancer

With the Advanced Manned Strategic Aircraft (AMSA) programme of the 1960s and early 1970s, it seemed that the United States was finally looking to find a replacement for the B-52 Stratofortress. The AMSA proposal accepted by the USAF was submitted to North American, which changed its name to Rockwell International and was given the designation B-1A for its new bomber design.

Rockwell had hoped to call the new bomber 'Excalibur', after King Arthur's sword, but the name was disapproved because it was also the name of a popular brand of condom. A decision to purchase was made on 5 June 1970, this in due course giving rise to the roll-out of the gleaming white B-1A bomber (serial 74-0159), taken for its first flight from Palmdale to Edwards AFB, California, by Charles Bock on 23 December 1974. Four development aircraft were built and SAC proceeded with plans to procure 240 production B-1A, the first to enter service in 1979. The B-1A programme proceeded with much support from Congress and all concerned, and seemed inevitable to come to fruition. Although much smaller than the B-52, the B-1A could carry 50 per cent more payload at nearly twice the speed. It seemed that all SAC's aspirations as to the future strategic bomber had been met. The aircraft was powered by four 29,900lb thrust General Electric F101-GE-100 engines, which made it not only fast but exceedingly powerful. As a public relations gesture, on 19 April 1976, Defence Secretary Donald Rumsfield (President Ford's right hand man) took the controls to fly the B-1A at 1,448 km/h (900 mph).

With all the euphoria surrounding the new strategic bomber, it hardly seemed creditable when a new administration took office, that of President Jimmy Carter and on 30 June 1977 cancelled the B-1A programme. Especially after the same company's XB-70 had also been cancelled. There seemed little prospect that SAC would ever get a next-generation strategic bomber. With the cancellation, SAC 'top brass' became convinced they would have to settle for an improved version of the FB-111A Aardvark fighter-bomber, to be known as the FB-111H

However, when President Reagan took office on 20 January 1981, B-1A testing resumed under the Long Range Combat Aircraft (LRCA) project. In October 1981, the Reagan administration revived the B-1 programme and announced plans to build 100 aircraft with improved features, the aircraft now designated B-1B. This was a long way short of the original 240-aircraft USAF requirement, but SAC commanders were pleased they were to get some new bomber equipment.

The B-1B differed from the B1A primarily on the following: the drastic reduction in radar cross-section from the equivalent of 10 square metres for the B-1A to 1.45 square metres for the B-1B through the use of radar-absorbent material (RAM) and careful attention to producing smooth contoured unbroken external surfaces ; a redesigned over-wing fairing ; re-engineered engine nacelles with fixed instead of variable inlets ; fitment of slightly more powerful F101-GE-101 engines instead of F101-GE-100s ; increase in gross weight from 395,000 to 477,000lb (the increase including an additional 24,000lb of fuel and 8,000lb of additional structures.; modified weapons bays to carry a greater variety of stores including the new ALCMs as well as conventional 'free-fall' bombs. ; increased weapons load (for example 72 Short-Range Attack Missiles - SRAMs instead of 24) ; ejection seats in place of the crew-escape capsule.

Performance changes included: maximum level speed at 15,240 metres (50,000ft) was reduced from Mach 2.0 (2,125 km/h or 1,320 mph) for the B-1A to Mach 1.25 (1,330 km/h or 835 mph) for the B-1B, while maximum penetration speed at 150 metres (500ft) was increased from Mach 0.85 (1,040 km/h or 647 mph) to Mach 0.92 (1,125 km/h or 700 mph); maximum unrefuelled range was increased from 9,815 km to 11,990 km (6,100 to 7,455 miles)

This good news for SAC, was also tainted with bad news: the second B-1A was lost on 29 August 1984 in California's Mojave Desert and although the crew ejected using the integral escape capsule, pilot Douglas Benefield was killed and two USAF officers injured. It was determined that the loss was not caused by any structural fault, and on 4 September 1984 the first B-1B (serial 82-0001) was rolled-out from the Rockwell plant and delivery of the first series aircraft took place in the summer of 1985. The type delivered to Offutt AFB, Nebraska, to be immediately re-assigned to the 96th Bomb Wing at Dyess AFB, Texas, for crew training of all SAC units earmarked to receive the new bomber. At this time the, 96th BW possessed two sub-ordinate echelons, the 337th Bomb Squadron (BS) and the 4018th Combat Crew Training Squadron (CCTS), although the latter proved fairly short-lived and was soon inactivated, with its training mission passed to the 338th CCTS so as to preserve USAF historical bomber unit links. The first operational squadron was the 337th Bombardment Squadron which had been equipped with B-52H until January 1985.

In due course the 96th BW too, suffered from the USAF's desire to link it current units with the past and it was inactivated on 1 October 1993, at which time responsibility for controlling the operations of the Dyess-based B-1B force passed to the 7th Wing. The subsequent unit re-organisation involving quite a complex number of de-activations and re-activations, that continued into 1994, with a number of B-52G and H units transitioning to form four B-1B Wings, that kept their aircraft, readied and armed ready to launch and execute the emergency 'war order' in a matter of minutes should the need arise.

With the end of the Cold War stand-off the possibility of nuclear war between East and West receded in the early 1990s and President George Bush Snr. seized the opportunity to order a stand-down of the long-running 'alert' programme during a nationwide television address on 17 September 1991.

Less than 24 hours later, munitions experts at a dozen bases in the United States finished the job of removing nuclear weapons from a force of about 40 B-1B Lancers and B-52 Stratofortresses and for the first time in almost 34 years no manned bombers stood on ground alert.

The B-1Bs early career was blighted by at least half-a-dozen instances of grounding, as well as difficulties with its complex AN/ALQ-161 defensive avionics suite. Indeed, although it took no part in Gulf War 1 in 1991, it was actually grounded on two occasions during the course of *Desert Shield* — and therefore automatically became unavailable. Engine-related problems were responsible on both occasions, but the second instance was of rather greater duration, beginning on 19 December 1990 and extending until 6 February 1991. With by now the B-52G Stratofortress bearing the brunt of operations in the Gulf. The unfortunate B-1 bearing the stigma of being the only major American combat plane not to take part in the conflict.

In addition, the end of the Cold War almost overnight negated the reason for the bombers existence. For the B-1 had primarily been created to bolster the United States nuclear deterrent capability, while at the same time furnishing SAC with a formidable conventional bombing capability. The latter to become the major premise of the bomber under the auspices of its new commanders by way of Air Combat Command (ACC) that superseded SAC in the early 1990s. Although the Lancer is still nuclear capable.

The B model used blended wing/body shape and relatively simple air inlet ducts in place of the variable-geometry intakes once preferred for the type, with variable-geometry 'swing-wings' an inherent feature (as with many other designs of the era). The B-1Bs outer wing panels have 15° of leading edge sweep when cranked forward for low-speed flight and landing; 59° when fully-swept for supersonic flight. The B-1B employs an SMCS (Structural Mode Control System) to minimise the effect of turbulence on crew and airframe during high-speed, low-level penetration of enemy airspace.

The four-man crew of the B-1B comprise; aircraft commander (AC), co-pilot, offensive systems operator and defensive systems operator. Unlike the cramped B-52, the B-1B offers bunks on the cabin floor for rest on long intercontinental missions and a much needed toilet. The original B-1A was designed with three tandem bomb-bays each 15ft long and able to house a bomb-load of up to 25,000lb. When the B-1B entered service, the bomb-bay had been re-designed to accommodate the AGM-86B cruise missile, which supplanted the AGM-69A short-range attack missile (SRAM) prominent in the B-52 force. In the B-1B a single bay 40ft in length can accommodate six ALCMs and four under-fuselage hard-points can be added.

Rather surprisingly for such a superb aircraft, the B-1 has received a considerable amount of bad press. It has been criticised for everything from not flying high enough to not having a HUD (Head-Up Display). It is true, of course, that the bombers service ceiling of 26,000ft is far from impressive and leaves it extremely vulnerable to SAMs. ."

Nevertheless, the aircraft was never intended for the high-altitude mission. "The thing about, the lack of a HUD makes no sense," according to Lt-Col Larry Nilssen. "The B-1B Lancers that sit on runway alert are already 'zipped up' (enclosed by thermal blast screens which eliminate outside visibility) before anyone ever gives the order to take off. We go into combat 'zipped'. A HUD would be useless

Although the B-1 has been the subject of great controversy, B-1B crews are convinced their mount is the best in the business — at least until the long-promised B-2A Spirit Advanced Technology 'stealth' Bomber (ATB) became a reality.

In 1989, the SAC bomber force comprised the Boeing B-52 Stratofortress, Rockwell B-1B Lancer and the General Dynamics FB-111A Aardvark.

Though the B-1 looks small. It is not. The B-1B is 44.81 metres (147ft) long and stands 10.36 metres (36ft 10in) high. It can carry 57 tons of bombs. It can fly 6,500 miles without refuelling. It takes a crew of four to operate it. As well as the pilot and co-pilot, there is the Offensive Systems Operator - a navigator/bomb aimer in old parlance — and a Defensive Systems Operator. The crew enters the aircraft via the belly hatch immediately behind the nose-wheel, equipped with its own retractable ladder. To save vital minutes under SAC's rapid response programme, the 'Start' switch for the Auxiliary Power Unit is mounted on the nose-wheel strut. The first crew member to reach the airplane hits the switch. By the time the four crew members are ensconced in the cockpit, the systems are powered-up and ready. Under 'alert' conditions, power-up and settling-in is supposed to take three minutes or less.

The bomber has a very spacious cockpit. The two system operators sit side-by-side behind the pilots, and there was provision for two instructor's seats, too. Not ejector seats, in an emergency the instructors would have to exit the airplane through the main hatch (if possible !). The four B-1B crew have individual ACES II (Aircraft Common Escape System) state-of-the-art ejection seats as fitted in the F-16 fighter, unlike the original B-1A that had a capsule arrangement like the F-111.

Right from the outset, the B-1 was to be a very long range aircraft, capable of thirty-six hour missions, and so it was necessary to provide a reasonable amount of crew comfort. There is room to stand and stretch, perhaps to do a few simple exercises to keep the body subtle. There is also a miniscule galley where drinks and pre-packed meals can be prepared and heated, and a chemical toilet. One of the items on the pre-landing check-list is "dump the contents of the chemical toilet..."
Of the skills needed to fly the B-1B, the pilots themselves agree that it is in a different league from its predecessors. If the first generation of long-range bombers needed warriors to fly them, and the next flyers, the B-1 is for the technocrats, the gadget freaks. The person that makes the best B-1 pilot is the 'tinkerer', the type who spent his or her childhood looking for things to fix. The airplane is nothing more than a collection of complex mechanical, electronic and structural sub-systems.

The bomber is relatively conventional as far as flying functions are concerned, the main exception the wing geometry. Ground manoeuvres, take-off and landing are performed with the wings set at minimum sweep of 15°. In fact the pilot cannot lower the flaps when the wings are swept at more than 20°.

On the ground the bomber is stiff and slow to respond to the controls, partly because the landing gear was designed that way, and partly because the flight surfaces are hydraulically operated, but that changes abruptly on the take-off run. Under wartime conditions there are abbreviated ways of getting into the air fast, but under normal circumstances, B-1B take-off is very much like that of a commercial airliner except that the afterburner is used.

The B-1B is flown like a fighter aircraft, with the stick and the rudder pedals. The aircraft was originally conceived for deep penetration and strategic bombardment of targets deep inside the Soviet Union, should the US National Command Authority decide to implement the Single Integrated Operations Plan. That meant navigating a trans-polar route, with several refuelling from KC-135 or KC-10 tankers, going into the combat phase of the mission at very low level, and flying cross country at less than 200ft using all the hi-tech miracles that have been incorporated into the Offensive Avionics System to take care of navigation, targeting, bomb delivery, defence, stores management and terrain-following. All at ten miles per minute.

For long-range nuclear attack the B-1B carries eight AGM-86B/C cruise missiles in the forward weapons bay. Fourteen more can be carried externally. The maximum conventional load is either 38 Mk 84 2,000lb bombs or 128 Mk 82 500lb weapons. For tactical nuclear attack, up to 38 AGM-69 SRAM can be carried, 24 internally and the rest on the external pylons.

To maximise the load it can carry, the B-1B's bomb-bay can be fitted with either rotary bomb/missile carriers, or sleeves that work in just the same way as a clip of rifle ammunition. A typical maximum conventional bomb-load is twenty-four 500lb Mk 82s, fitted with ballutes (half balloon, half parachute) to retard them.

While the B-1 has fighter like controls it cannot be flown like a fighter and thrown all over the skies. The airframe has restrictions for sustained rate of roll and for inverted flight. Inside it is like being in a spacecraft more than an 150 ton bomber.

In actual combat, the B-1B would attack more than one target. Things like missile silos, rail checkpoints, garrisons, airbases, naval bases, and communications centres etc. Only fuel would limit endurance and the number of targets to be hit, as there is no way in-flight refuelling tankers could venture over enemy airspace. The bomber would recover from enemy territory low and fast making full use of the terrain-following technology in the hope of rendezvousing with a AAC tanker in friendly airspace.

The B-1 is landed in a straightforward manner, much like the Boeing F-15 Eagle strike fighter. Airbraking is performed by the large horizontal stabiliser. There is no brake chute. All equipment deficiencies and malfunctions monitored by the aircrafts computer and built-in-test equipment, are recorded for examination and rectification by the ground crews later.

In the early 1990s, the B-1B had an appalling 55 per cent mission-capable rate, in the main due to supply and support issues. At one time, each airframe of the 100 aircraft built, had a separate supply manual. When the type made its first overseas trip to appear at the Paris Air Salon in June 1987, the aircraft was grounded with an embarrassing 76-hour maintenance 'glitch' while the aviation press took notes and cameras took endless photographs.

So troublesome was the bomber's defensive electronics system that a Washington periodical dubbed the B-1B 'the world's first self-jamming bomber'. In August 1991, the USAF acknowledged that 14 aircraft had developed cracks in the 25° aileron, requiring a 'fix' at a cost of $50,000 per aircraft. Worse still an August 1991, a study by the Institute for Defence Analysis determined that plans to retrofit a scaled-down version of the defensive aids system would not enable the bomber to defeat the Soviet defences. Soon afterwards, the commitment of the B-1B to the SIOP - the Single Integrated Operations Plan, which prescribes strategy, tactics, and targeting for the early hours of an atomic war — ended. The B-1B Lancer no longer had a nuclear mission.

The aircraft continued to be the subject of derision and the USAF grounded the 'Bone' ('B-one') several times due to safety considerations. Configured only for nuclear weapon delivery in 1990/91, there was no practical reason to use the aircraft in Gulf War I in operation *Desert Storm*, though the pressure was enormous for the bomber to make a public appearance in combat. In the end the USAF did not have sufficient confidence in the airplane to deploy it to the Gulf — and in any case as already related it was grounded — due to engine problems ! It was a worrying situation for an airplane that was supposed to represent the future for ACC's bomber force.

The change to conventional bombing capability came soon after the war. Once the press and public ceased its continued lambasting of the airplane, as mission capability and readiness improved sharply the USAF brought the bomber up to Block C standard with the capability to carry CBU-87/89/97 cluster bombs. The B-1B force reached RAA (Required Assets Available), a term that replaced IOC (Initial Operating Capability) in Block C when three aircraft of the 37th Bomb Squadron at Ellsworth AFB, South Dakota, became combat-ready with cluster bombs in September 1996. By this time most of the supply, maintenance and logistics problems had been resolved.

By the end of the decade the 'Bone' had been brought to Block D status, which provides the B-1B with GPS (Global Positioning System), communications improvements, and the ALE-50 towed decoy. The first Block D-configured airplane (serial 85-0068) was delivered from the Rockwell factory at Palmdale, California, to Edwards AFB, California, in March 1997. RAA status was reached two years later, in March 1999.

In the course of its operational service, several B-1s have been lost in mishaps. In 1996, Dyess-based B-1B serial 86-0106 crashed after a night low-level flight just after leaving the Sierra Vieja Mountains. The four crew members were killed instantly. For an unknown reason the crew allegedly disconnected the terrain-following during an automatic steep climb to clear a ridge and a few seconds later the Lancer collided head-on with a mountain wall. Analysis of the flight data recorder indicated that everything had been functioning normally. It is of interest serial 86-0106 had survived an earlier accident when in a mid-air collision with a KC-135R tanker over Nebraska on 24 March 1992. Some reports relate that 86-0106 was written-off as a resulted of the collision, when in fact it landed safely and was repaired, only to be written-off in 1996.

Later, in 1998, another Dyess AFB, B-1B (serial 85-0063) was lost due to a malfunctioning fire warning/fire extinguisher control panel. Fortunately all four crew members ejected successfully.

The most tragic mishap, occurred on 28 September 1987, the result of a bird strike over the La Junta Radar Bomb site in New Mexico. The aircraft (serial 84-0052) had two additional instructors aboard seated on jump seats. As the aircraft became uncontrollable, and the rest of the ejection seated crew waited as long as they could, the two instructors were unable to open the crew entrance hatch to egress and parachute to safety. The co-pilot's seat failed to leave the aircraft as well, and three fatalities resulted. Jump seats are no longer used, and changes in low-level training routes have been made to minimise the chances of another such incident.

In the meantime, the bomber, attired in its 'penetrator grey' colour scheme, redeemed itself when used for the first time on combat operations over Iraq during Operation *Desert Fox* in December 1998.

Without guns or missiles the Lancer relies on a combination of armed escort and mission tactics to avoid enemy defensive systems. Deployment of chaff and flares assist in defensive matters, and the aircraft can deploy the ALE-50 towed decoy. The ALE-50 was utilised by B-1s in combat over Yugoslavia during the Spring of 1999. The decoy transmits an electronic signal stronger than the actual radar reflection from the bomber. The USAF stated that the ten surface-to-air missiles (SAMs) that locked-on to B-1s attacking Yugoslav airfields were all diverted by the ALE-50.

Further upgrades has brought the B-1 to Block E standard fitted with a new computer and the WCMD (Wind-Corrected Munitions Dispenser), The upgrades commensurate with the CMUP (Conventional Munitions Upgrade Program).

Since the take-over of Rockwell, the B-1B Lancer has undergone a Boeing $2.16 billion conventional mission upgrade. The airplanes have received anti-jam radios, GPS navigation and a 1760-databus weapons capability. The depot level modifications were due to be completed in 2003. Further planned enhancements include a PC-based avionics computer and modular core software by 2005; and the General Weapons Interface System, providing the ability for the bomber to carry a mixed load of WCMDs, JSOWs and JASSMs.

A planned Block F programme upgrade was cancelled in 2002. But, a proposed Block G upgrade is scheduled to cover fifteen items, including the addition of Link 16 and beyond-line-of-sight satcom datalink, cockpit modernisation and radar upgrade.

Boeing would like to fit seven or eight commercial MFDs, militarised for NVGs. This would enable moving map and tactical data to be displayed at any crew station, while an interactive attack planner would enable the crew to replan the mission in-flight. Fitment of new processors would upgrade the Northrop Grumman APQ-144 radar. Boeing has also proposed an electronic warfare version.

It is of interest that, although the variable wing-sweep bomber can fly in any configuration between 15° and 67.5°, the vast majority of missions are flown in three positions 15°, 25° and 67.5°. The latter for high-speed supersonic - Mach 1.2 - flight.

A programme to install Lockheed Martin's Sniper XR targeting pod for target identification and weapon deployment is being considered with the first trials flight planned for 2006. The USAF is also exploring the possibility of installing defensive aid 'laser cannons' and has conducted computer simulations of this new weapon, which would be used to defeat air and ground missile threats.

In 2006, of the slimmed-down fleet of operational B-1B Lancers, some 36 are 'combat coded' (i. e. kept combat ready), while the other twenty-four are in training status, depot maintenance or assigned to test duties. In 2006, the B-1Bs *lifed* at 15,200 hrs cannot last beyond 2029 at their, airframe hours usage of 420 per year.

During Operation *Iraqi Freedom* - Gulf War II in 2003, the eleven bombers deployed attacked one third of the targets in only five percent of the sorties. Throughout the conflict at least one B-1B was in the air around the clock, ready to engage emerging targets with precision guided weapons. One of these airplanes of the 405th Expeditionary Wing, operating from Thumrait in Oman, was called forward to attack a building near Baghdad thought to be housing Saddam Hussein, but, the Iraqi dictator had fled by the time of the attack.

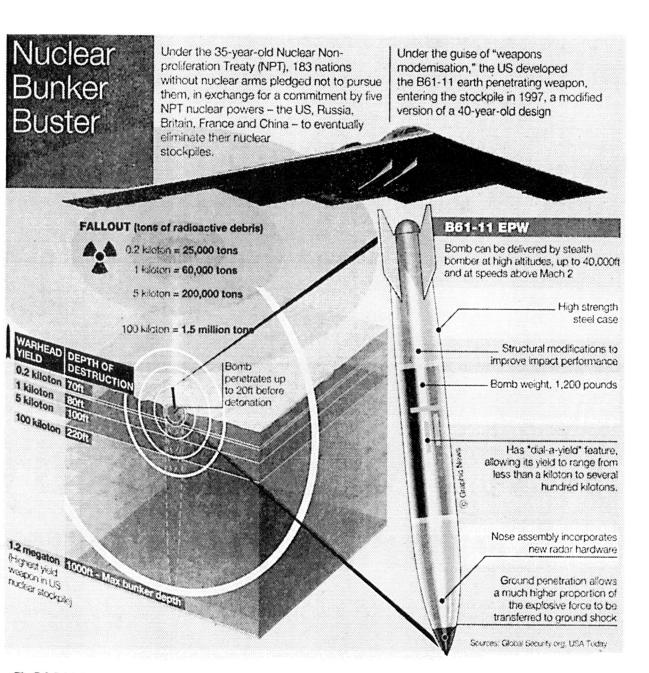

Nuclear Bunker Buster

Under the 35-year-old Nuclear Non-proliferation Treaty (NPT), 183 nations without nuclear arms pledged not to pursue them, in exchange for a commitment by five NPT nuclear powers – the US, Russia, Britain, France and China – to eventually eliminate their nuclear stockpiles.

Under the guise of "weapons modernisation," the US developed the B61-11 earth penetrating weapon, entering the stockpile in 1997, a modified version of a 40-year-old design

FALLOUT (tons of radioactive debris)

0.2 kiloton = 25,000 tons

1 kiloton = 60,000 tons

5 kiloton = 200,000 tons

100 kiloton = 1.5 million tons

WARHEAD YIELD	DEPTH OF DESTRUCTION
0.2 kiloton	70ft
1 kiloton	80ft
5 kiloton	100ft
100 kiloton	220ft
1.2 megaton (Highest yield weapon in US nuclear stockpile)	1000ft = Max bunker depth

Bomb penetrates up to 20ft before detonation

B61-11 EPW

Bomb can be delivered by stealth bomber at high altitudes, up to 40,000ft and at speeds above Mach 2

High strength steel case

Structural modifications to improve impact performance

Bomb weight, 1,200 pounds

Has "dial-a-yield" feature, allowing its yield to range from less than a kiloton to several hundred kilotons.

Nose assembly incorporates new radar hardware

Ground penetration allows a much higher proportion of the explosive force to be transferred to ground shock

© Graphic News

Sources: Global Security.org, USA Today

The B-2 Spirit is to be the carrier for the B61-11 EPW — Earth Penetrating Weapon — flying at altitudes up to 40,000ft at speeds up to Mach 2.0.

87.

Chapter 12   Strategic Air Command (SAC) & Air Combat Command (ACC)

Much of the credit for building the mighty SAC force belongs to General Curtiss E LeMay, who was its Commander from 1948 to 1957. Under LeMay's leadership, SAC's personnel strength rose from 51,965 to 224,014 and the total number of aircraft on inventory from 837 to 2,711.

SAC's B-36 and B-47 bombers belonged to a time when jet engines lacked the fuel efficiency needed for strategic operations against the Soviet Union. Thus, the prop-driven B-36 Peacemaker had to retain the 'heavy' bomber role long after the jet-powered Boeing B-47 was in service, the latter being classed a medium bomber. In the 1950s, SAC had no greater priority than the creation of a true 'heavy' all-jet bomber force. This was achieved with the Boeing B-52 Stratofortress, which was created under enormous pressure, making its first flight in 1952, and entered service in 1955. Seen as an 'interim' solution for perhaps about eight years or so, the B-52 has ended up being one of the longest serving combat aircraft of all time.

A spirit of innovation persisted into the 1950s. The USAF toyed with the Martin XB-53, a jet bomber with forward-swept wings (FSW) : ahead of its time, the concept was tested three decades later in the ultra high-tech Grumman X-29 research aircraft, that also did not enter series production. At the same time the reciprocating engine refused to go away and SAC evaluated the Boeing B-54, an updated and extensively rebuilt version of the proven B-50. Neither the XB-53 nor the B-54 got very far, but there were plenty of fresh ideas put forward to keep SAC commander General E LeMay equipped with new hardware for his all-powerful Strategic Air Command.

As new plans for the late 1950s were made, it was conceivable that the back-bone of SAC's striking power might become the Boeing XB-55, medium bomber on Boeing's drawing board as the intended replacement for the B-47 Stratojet. One of several Boeing designs at the time, much of the nations thinking on advanced bomber development lay with the Seattle-based Boeing engineering team, where soft-spoken Edward C Wells stood out as an extraordinary design expert and leader. Pencil sketches made by Wells led to the Boeing 474, swept-wing, turbo-prop aircraft which looked if anything a step backwards from the jet powered B-47 (and reverted to the WW II practice of locating a tail gunner in a rear fuselage turret). Once it became apparent that SAC were not particularly enthused with turbo-prop engines for their strategic bombers (though the Soviets were perfectly happy to use them on their Tupolev Tu-95/Tu-142 'Bear' Series), this design was assimilated into the XB-55 (Boeing Model 479), where power was provided by six J40 turbojet engines.

The XB-55 won approval by a SAC review board and might well have joined the SAC bomber force of the late 1950s, whose inventory grew to more than 2,500 aircraft. But before an order could be placed or metal cut, another design from Wells' brilliant team came into the spotlight and rendered every other bomber design of the era obsolete. The XB-52 Stratofortress (Boeing Model 464-67) was born.

In the 1950s, the United States relied almost exclusively on its heavy bombers to deter Soviet communist global ambitions. The B-52 made it truly possible for USAF bombers to attack anywhere in the world. This capability was demonstrated in November 1956, when eight B-52Bs from the 93rd Heavy Bombardment Wing at Castle AFB, California, made a 27,300 km (17,000 mile) flight around North America over the North Pole, being continuously airborne for thirty-two hours. On 16/17 January 1957, when three SAC B-52s, commanded by Major General Archie J. Olds, flew non-stop around the world, having been refuelled in flight three times, covering 24,235 miles in 45 hours 19 minutes. Once the B-52 was actually in service, beginning with the 93rd Bomb Wing at Castle AFB from June 1956, it remained only for the Boeing KC-135 Stratotanker (first flight: 31 August 1956) to support the Stratofortresses global missions at jet speeds.

By the time General LeMay left to turn over his beloved SAC to General Thomas S Power on 1 July 1957, the fiercely disciplined 'hard' crews of the B-52s could carry nuclear weapons on long-range 'alert' missions almost totally impervious from intercept by the Soviet Union's MiG fighters.
The readiness of a poised force of SAC bombers, including up to 500 B-52s, undoubtedly helped United States policy interests throughout the world troubles of the 1950s and early 1960s — the Taiwan Straits, the Berlin Wall, and the Cuban Missile Crisis.

Strategic Air Command (SAC), Tactical Air Command (TAC), and Military Air Command (MAC) disappeared on 1 June 1992, all three were formally dis-established with their inventories re-distributed between two new newly created commands. These were the Air Combat Command (ACC) and Air Mobility Command (AMC), respectively headquartered at Langley AFB, Virginia and Scott AFB, Illinois. Under General John M Loh, ACC assumed responsibility for all TAC's combat planes, as well as all strategic bombers, missile and reconnaissance units previously under SAC control. AMC, headed by General H. T. Johnson, acquired the transport assets of MAC, and most, but not all of SAC's large fleet of in-flight KC-135 and KC-10 refuelling tankers. Overseas-based units (Air Forces) assumed command over former SAC, MAC and TAC elements within their specific areas of responsbility. As for example the 435th Airlift Wing based at Rhein-Main, Germany, now reported to USAFE rather than MAC as has previously been the case. Overall the re-organisation saw the number of active air force personnel reduced from 570,000 to 400,000, although there were more than 301,000 in the Air National Guard (ANG) and Air Force Reserve (AFres). At the same time a new organisation was created, namely, Air Force Material Command (AFMC), responsible for the development, acquisition, delivery and operational support of air force weapons systems. This was achieved by the merger of Air Force Logistics Command and Air Force Systems Command, on 1 July 1992.

In terms of budget the re-organisation of the USAF reduced the cost to the American taxpayers from a high of $94.685 billion in fiscal year 1989 to $71.881 billion by 1996. Not surprisingly the overall number of airplanes available dropped from 9,279 in fiscal year 1989 to 6,633 in 1995.

With regard to active duty types this represented a decline in bomber strength from 412 to 183, in tankers from 578 to 325, in fighter/interceptor/attack planes from 2,896 to 1,750, in reconnaissance/ electronic warfare from 416 to 318, in cargo/transport from 825 to 690, in fixed wing search and rescue from 35 to 12, in helicopters (incuding rescue) from 205 to 123, in trainers from 1,540 to 1,205 and in utility, communications, observation etc, from 140 to 104. Between fiscal year 1991 and fiscal year 1996, the number of flying squadrons (including ANG and AFres) declined from 401 to 360.

SAC & ACC US BOMBER FLEETS

Headquartered at Barksdale AFB, Louisiana, under a re-organisation implemented in September 1991, the US 8th Air Force was given control of all operational B-1B Lancers and B-52G/H Stratofortresses assigned to Strategic Air Command (SAC). These were flown by thirteen flying wings, all of which also operated the Boeing KC-135 Stratotanker, although these were accountable to the 15th Air Force. Prior to the re-organisation, the 8th Air Force administered SAC operations on the eastern half of the United States along with many of the northern states and in Europe; while the 15th Air Force at March AFB, California controlled units on the western side and the Pacific.

Formed during the dark days of WW II initially to undertake dangerous B-17 Flying Fortress day – bomber raids on Germany, since 1945, the 8th Air Force has played a significant part in all major USAF actions, including the significant contribution as a peacetime deterrent force during the Cold War with the Soviet Union.

In June 1950, North Korean forces invaded the South and amongst those US air force units deployed to the region were the SAC Boeing B-29 Groups from the 2nd and 15th Air Forces, while the 8th Air Force provided Republic F-84E Thunderjets from the 27th Fighter Wing which deployed to Taegu. At the time the 8th comprised seven Wings, consisting of two F-84Es, one with Convair RB-36 reconnaissance bombers, two with B-36 bombers, and two with a mix of Boeing B-50s and Boeing KP-29P in-flight refuellers. After initial setbacks in Korea the UN lead offensive prevailed and an uneasy peace returned to the still (in 2006) divided country.

As the first jet bombers began entering SAC service in the early 1950s, by way of the Boeing B-47 Stratojet, the 8th Air Force began receiving its first examples. The expansion of SAC at this time was enormous with units switching to jet bombers at a rapid rate. Apart from the Wings located in the comparative safety of the northern and central states, there was a build up of units in the north-east corner of the country, as these were in a primary position to retaliate against any Soviet pre-emptive strike.

SAC re-organised its structure on 13 June 1955 with the 8th Air Force moving to Westover AFB, Massachusetts. The change still left SAC units largely responsible for geographical regions, with the 8th managing the north-east and part of the central region, while the 2nd Air Force was tasked with Texas and the south-east and the 15th Air Force with the far west. Of the fifteen wings forming the 8th Air Force in 1956, four were dedicated to strategic reconnaissance, operating RB-47E/H Stratojets, seven were equipped with B-47B/E jet bombers and one each with the new Boeing B-52C and D models of the Stratofortress. All of these units were assigned a single Air Refuelling Squadron operating Boeing KC-97 piston-engined tankers.

On 1 January 1959, the 8th formed the 702nd Strategic Missile Wing at Presque Isle AFB, Maine, as the first unit to be assigned the SM-62 Snark intercontinental missile (ICM). This was the first time that missile and bomber forces had been integrated in this way. The project was plagued with problems but despite requests by SAC that the weapon be cancelled, the Snark Wing was eventually declared operational in February 1961.

However, the writing was already on the wall, and with the Snark already considered to be obsolete and of little military value, the Wing became a victim of the defence budget cuts just four months later.

Development of more capable missile systems had continued throughout the 1950s with the Atlas programme becoming the first operational Intercontinental Ballistic Missile (ICBM) at the end of the decade. At the same time the Mk 1 version of the Titan missile was being readied for service as another of the first generation ICBMs. The 8th Air Force did not receive ICBMs until 1962, with the first Titan 1 unit becoming operational during the Cuban Missile crisis. As the 1960s progressed SAC continued its modernisation and early versions of the B-52 Stratofortress was joined by later models.

Throughout this period SAC rotated entire Wings to bases overseas to act as a deterrent to Soviet communist intentions and be in a more advantageous position to respond to any aggressive actions if necessary. While the air force was prepared to move units to Europe across the Atlantic or in the opposite direction across the Pacific if necessary for a 90-day rotation period this was disruptive to the smooth running of the home base and brought about numerous difficulties to day-to-day home-based operations. Instead, the *Reflex Action* system was evaluated, whereby small numbers of bombers from several units were detached to their overseas location for three weeks before being relieved in a constantly rotating pattern. The system proved highly successful and was implemented as Wings completed their 90-day overseas assignments in 1958. The 8th Air Force has the distinction of being the last unit to perform a 90-day tour of the UK when the 100th Bomb Wing returned to Pease AFB, New Hampshire from RAF Brize Norton, Oxon, in April 1958.

Subsequently, the threat posed by the Soviet Union's growing number of ICBMs necessitated a change in the composition of SAC Wings. Several bases housed more than one wing with in excess of 100 bombers and tankers on base when all had returned from overseas locations. With most of the remainder, containing a Wing composed of three Bombardment Squadrons (BS) and a single Air Refuelling Squadron operating between 50 and 60 aircraft. While capable of supporting this number of aircraft, it was realised a surprise attack by Soviet ICBMs would in all probability result in many aircraft being destroyed on the ground. The solution was seen as the same as used by the RAF's V-Force in the UK, dispersal. In this way the fleet was dispersed in smaller numbers at bases across the USA to make Soviet targeting more difficult. This permitted more bombers and tankers to take-off in the short amount of early warning time available (at this time, considered to be about 15 minutes). To this end the number of bases available to the air force increased considerably, which in the case of the 8th Air Force resulted in no fewer than 26 facilities supporting SAC operations by the early 1960s. Apart from home bases, additional facilities in Greenland and Canada were used to support SAC operations regularly.

The final B-52 an H model was delivered to SAC in October 1962 while the last KC-135A jet-powered tanker was accepted in 1964. 1966 saw the final B-47E Stratojet and KC-97G retired from service with the 8th Air Force. As the new equipment continued to arrive, SAC bomber presence in Europe was gradually reduced during the first half of the 1960s as *Reflex Action* ceased. As the United States sent increasing numbers of military forces to south-east Asia, SAC *Arc Light* Stratofortress operations launched from Andersen AFB, Guam were initially restricted to the B-52F model drawn from units outside the 8th Air Force, although their bomb carrying capability was limited. However, during the Spring of 1966 the B-52F was replaced by the B-52D deployed from 28th and 484th Bomb Wings. The latter unit being part of the 8th Air Force, with its aircraft converted by the 'Big Belly' modifications to double their bomb carrying capability. The 4133rd Bomb Wing (Provisional) was formed at Andersen to operate the bombers, while U-Tapao RTAFB, Thailand began operating B-52D in the Spring of 1967 under the 4258th Strategic Wing (SW) and later the 307th Strategic Wing.

Nine B-52D Wings rotated aircraft to carry out combat operations over Vietnam including two, from the 8th Air Force, consisting of the 306th BW from McCoy AFB, Florida and 484th BW at Turner AFB, Georgia. The requirement for additional tanker operations necessitated an increase in the number of bases available to SAC with tankers based at U-Tapao and Kadena AB, Okinawa supplemented by those rotated periodically to Clark AB, Philippines and Ching Chuan Kang AB, Taiwan.

B-52D operations also increased with additional aircraft deploying to Kadena AB in 1968 for the 4252nd Strategic Wing and later the 307th Strategic Wing. The bombing campaign continued until 1969 when a steady decline began and bombers began to return back to the United States. For sixteen years SAC operations had been administered at Andersen AFB by the 3rd Air Division until April 1970 when it was replaced by Headquarters 8th Air Force. Simultaneously the 43rd Strategic Wing was reactivated at Andersen to replace the 3960th Strategic Wing as the primary unit at the base. The 8th was relocated to the region primarily to control SAC activities in the region as the Command was reluctant to transfer operations to the Pacific Air Forces.

During 1972, reconnaissance of the Ho Chi Minh trail showed a concentration of weapons and supplies filtering southward and 8th Air Force B-52 sorties were stepped up from approximately 1,000 per month to more than three times this number, although an additional forty-two aircraft stationed at U-Tapao were found inadequate to meet this increase in operations. Twenty-nine additional B-52Ds were deployed from the United States to Andersen AFB in February 1972, and were followed by additional batches later, including substantial numbers of B-52Gs. U-Tapao had 50 B-52Ds in residence by mid-1972, while Andersen had a massive complement of 150 B-52D and G Models. Continued operations against the Ho Chi Minh trail halted the flow of supplies into South Vietnam, permitting the Stratofortresses to switch their attention to the bombing of industrial complexes in North Vietnam under Operation *Linebacker* which ended in late October.

Peace negotiations in Paris continued without progress, and it was the continued bombing of the North under the auspices of *Linebacker II* that was used to press home the fact that America was determined to bring the conflict to a conclusion.

An intense and sustained 12-day aerial assault by numerous B-52 Stratofortresses against targets in Hanoi and Haiphong were flown during the latter half of December 1972, that finally brought about a ceasefire agreement from the North Vietnamese.

Bombing of the North ceased on 15 January 1973 while operations over south Vietnam continued until the ceasefire came into effect on 27 January. 8th Air Force B-52 operations continued over Laos until the 17 April, while the last sortie over Cambodia took place on 15 August 1973. The Paris agreement permitted the large B-52 force in South-East Asia to be reduced with aircraft returning home throughout 1973. Likewise the large fleet of in-flight refuelling tankers used to support the war also decreased

The much-reduced SAC presence in the Far East no longer required the presence of a numbered Air Force, and the 8th was relocated without equipment or personnel, to Barksdale AFB on 1 January 1975, to replace the 2nd Air Force. At the same time the 3rd Air Division was reactivated to fill the void left by the transfer home of the 8th. Back in the United States the 8th resumed control of SAC assets located along the eastern half of the USA and at Carswell AFB, Texas, while the 15th Air Force continued to be responsible for all other SAC units. Eighteen major units were under the 8th Air Force control while the 15th had a similar composition. Amongst the equipment inherited by the 8th was 60 FB-111A Aardvark strategic bombers split between the 380th and 509th Bomb Wings, six B-52 Wings, one unit operating the B-52D and two B-52H Wings, both located in Michigan. Of the remaining units, three were equipped with missiles (one with Minuteman II and two with Titan II), while the final three were equipped with KC-135A Stratotankers.

The remaining Titan missiles were removed from service in 1987 with the three missile wings of the 8th Air Force re-equipped with Minuteman II and III. The Rockwell B-1B Lancer entered service in 1987, with two Wings deploying those aircraft available for front-line operations. The McDonnell-Douglas KC-10A Extender tanker/transport entered service with two of the three units under the control of the 8th, although the 68th Air Refuelling Wing was deactivated in April 1991, when its 19 airplanes were transferred from SAC to TAC. Six of the 12 tanker units were upgraded to the Boeing KC-135R.

Although the B-1B was not involved in Gulf War 1 Operation *Desert Storm*, the 8th Air Force had a large contingency with all of its KC-135 and KC-10 units involved. Likewise B-52Gs were drawn almost exclusively from 8th Air Force units with the 2nd, 42nd, 97th, 379th and 416th Bomb Wings deploying to Moron, Spain, RAF Fairford in the UK, Jeddah, Saudi Arabia and Diego Garcia in the Indian Ocean. This was in the main due to the availability of the B-52G variant with its conventional bombing capability.

Subsequently, the mission of the 8th Air Force has remained largely unchanged, despite the introduction of new weapons systems - to command and operate aircraft, missiles and forces assigned by the Commander-in-Chief, SAC to the 8th Air Force to maintain a creditable airborne deterrent.

This has required the 8th to organise, train, equip and deploy numerous units to undertake conventional long-range bombing operations and airborne cruise missile launches and provide aerial tanker support as necessary in support of the various overseas deployments.

On 1 September 1991 SAC was re-organised from two to four numbered Air Forces and the allocation of units according to type (8th AF — bombers, 15th AF — tankers, 2nd AF — reconnaissance and 20th AF — missiles). The following year MAC (Military Airlift Command), SAC and TAC disappeared on 1 June when all three were formally dis-established with assets previously under their control being re-distributed between two newly-created commands. These were Air Combat Command (ACC) and Air Mobility Command (AMC) respectively headquartered at Langley AFB, Virginia and Scott AFB, Illinois. General John M Loh, - ACC, assumed responsibility for the 1st Air Force, 2nd AF, 8th AF (with most of the bomber assets), 9th AF, 12th AF, and the 20th Air Force ICBMs.

As the name suggests Air Combat Command has the primary role of strike and air defence with an area of responsibility encompassing not just the United States but also an overseas commitment with a rapid reaction force to deploy at short notice to bolster US forces in Europe, the Middle East, Asia and the Pacific. The Command became the sole operator of all SAC's bombers and reconnaissance aircraft plus approximately 20 percent of its tankers, the latter in six air refuelling squadrons. The remainder of SAC's tankers were assigned to AMC.

Former SAC bomber aircraft to join ACC include the B-1B Lancer, B-52G and H model Stratofortresses, plus the KC-135A and Q versions of the Stratotanker. The aircraft were finished in a new grey overall colour scheme wearing two letter identification codes. In addition their serial presentation changed to the tactical style with the fiscal year followed by the last three, e. g. 59-1471 presented as 91471 by SAC, changed to 59-471 with ACC.

Fourteen units had tail codes allocated, the majority of which represent the home base or state in which the base is located, although of course, as always there are exceptions to this rule.

Nine months before the command change was implemented, SAC changed the designation of its units which were equipped with bombers and tankers. These units simply became Wings with the role prefix eliminated. However, following transfer to ACC, those units which lost their tanker aircraft to AMC reverted to Bombardment Wing status.

Prior to formation of the two new Commands the Air Force had decided to drop the ultra-low visibility 'European One' colour scheme on transport, bombers and tankers in favour of mid-grey pattern. Freshly painted aircraft emerged from the Air Logistics Center in the new colour schemes following major servicing including, the B-1 and B-52 bombers, although with more than 2,000 large airplanes to paint this process, took several years to complete.

Appendix:

Air Expeditionary Forces - AEF's
Following experience gained by the needs of operations in conjunction with NATO in the Balkan and Kosovo conflicts, Air Expeditionary Forces have been created and it is from these units that the initial responses to world-wide operations will be drawn. The object, to maximise resources, and provide an immediate response and an ongoing state of readiness stateside with a rotation of units ensuring a fairer regime for those personnel called on to serve on the front-line, whereever and whenever that might be.

Designated AEF Lead Wings:

AEF	Wing	Location	Aircraft
AEF 1	388th Fighter Wing	Hill AFB, Utah	F-16CG/DG
AEF 2	7th Bomb Wing	Dyess AFB, Texas	B-1B
AEF 3	3rd Wing	Elmendorf AFB, Alaska	F-15C/D/E ; C-130H, E-3B/C
AEF 4	48th Fighter Wing	RAF Lakenheath, England	F-15C/D/E
AEF 5	355th Wing	Davis Monthan AFB, Arizona	OA/A-10A ; EC-130E/H
AEF 6	20th Fighter Wing	Shaw AFB, South Carolina	F-16CJ/DJ
AEF 7	2nd Bomb Wing	Barksdale AFB, Louisiana	B-52H
AEF 8	28th Bomb Wing	Ellsworth AFB, South Dakota	B-1B
AEF 9	27th Fighter Wing	Cannon AFB, New Mexico	F-16C/D
AEF 10	1st Fighter Wing	Langley AFB, Virginia	F-15C/D

Designated Mobility Lead Wings

AEF	Wing	Location	Aircraft
AEF 1/2	43rd Airlift Wing	Pope AFB, North Carolina	C-130E
AEF 3/4	60th Mobility Wing	Travis AFB, California	C-5A/B/C ; KC-10A
AEF 5/6	22nd ARF Wing	McConnell AFB, Kansas	KC-135R/T
AEF 7/8	319th ARF Wing	Grand Forks AFB, North Dakota	KC-135R/T
AEF 9/10	92nd ARF Wing	Fairchild AFB, Washington DC	KC-135R/T

USAF ACC strategic bomber inventory circa 2005/6

B1-B Lancer	60	(24 stored - 36 operational)
B-2A Spirit	21	(1 test work - 16 operational)
B-52H Stratofortress	84	(44 to be combat ready at any time)